UNSEEN BEINGS UNSEEN WORLDS

TOM DONGO

Copyright 1994 by Tom Dongo
ISBN 0-9622748-3-6

All rights reserved. No part of this book
may be reproduced by any means or in any form,
except brief quotes for literary reviews, without
written permission from the author.

Cover Design by
Tom Dongo and Fay Richards

Published by
Hummingbird Publishing
PO Box 2571
Sedona, AZ 86339

Printed by
Mission Possible Commercial Printing
a division of
Love Light Communication Services
PO Box 1526
Sedona, AZ 86336

Foreword

When I write a book I always have a number of people read copies of the manuscript before the book goes into print. These readers are carefully chosen by me from all age and interest levels and they often have diverse belief systems and spiritual backgrounds. This group can include anywhere between ten and twenty-five people. As a result of their comments I can get an assessment of the impact and marketability of a new book. It is a very accurate method.

I always get lots of honest, spontaneous and blunt feedback, and I always appreciate the comment, no matter what it is. A writer, to survive as a writer, must have a controllable ego and a very thick skin. I do. I always ask people to tell it like it is, and they do. If they like the book, I ask them to write in detail why. If they are indifferent to the book – tell me why. If they dislike the book – tell me why. Then, after reviewing and carefully considering the accumulated feedback, I can take another look at the manuscript and make any necessary changes. I can read a manuscript a hundred times and completely miss a glaring error or something essential that was left out or perhaps needs to be added, something another person often sees on the first reading.

About half of the people who read the manuscript of this book said it was excellent as it was but needed minor changes. An encouraging sign. The other half of the people who read it said it was good but certain things I'd written pushed their buttons. A couple of folks really had their buttons pushed! I am not and never have been one to sugar coat something excessively in order to gain someone's approval, a trait I think I proudly owe to my stoic, rather Puritanical, Maine Yankee upbringing. I come from a hard-nosed lot.

In a where-are-we-and-where-are-we-going sense, every single one of us is fishing for answers, *regardless of our backgrounds*. If we knew *the* Answers, we wouldn't be here. I have been intensely researching and experimenting with spiritual paths and paranormal occurrences for over ten years and I am admittedly just beginning to have a glimmering of what is going on.

Unseen Beings, Unseen Worlds

I think this book is important in a number of ways, but perhaps foremost is that prophesies such as those given by the seers Nostradamus, Edgar Cayce, and Gordon Michael Scallion, the apparition at Fatima, and the Bible, Pope John XXIII, the Hopi Prophecy and many others foretell of incredibly trying times in the *immediate* future of humankind. If these prophesies are right, and I think they are, then it will aid us enormously if we gain a more comfortable understanding of the nonphysical realms which await and surround us.

And, if we can openly communicate with our nonphysical counterparts we can perhaps gain knowledge and reassurance that would probably be obtainable in no other way. Direct and open contact I think is now a *clear probability* because of the enormity of what may lie in our paths. The dwellers of the spiritual and nonphysical (and alien) worlds are open and available to us—at least to those who look and who ask.

I didn't write this book with the deliberate intention of creating a fertile battleground for argument. We, as a race, argue and fight too much. Instead, we should collectively and cooperatively be searching for answers and solutions which will aid the whole of humankind. Writing a book about spiritual and paranormal activity is controversial at best and will inevitably, no matter how it's written, stampede across a few toes. With this book as with any information, you would do well to absorb what is of value to you and disregard the rest.

My fervent hope is that this book will spark interest in venturing beyond an accepted, perhaps questionable, reality and will launch a few fearless ships on a soaring journey into the wonderful and endlessly exciting realms of the Great Unknown.

Tom Dongo
Sedona, Arizona
1994

Contents

1	The Key to the Doorway	1
2	A Chorus of Voices in the Distance	11
3	The Astral Plane	23
4	The Light of the Creator Force	31
5	Another Strange Case of Possession	41
6	Uh Huh — A Ghost!	51
7	How to Talk to Spirits	61
8	How to Learn Remote Viewing	71
9	Meditation, Remote Viewing, Spontaneous Viewing and "Barriers"	81
10	The Wee People	87
11	ETs and Others	95
12	The Free Thinker and the Future	101
	Photograph Section	105

Unseen Beings, Unseen Worlds

God has placed in each soul an apostle to lead us upon the illumined path. Yet many seek life from without, unaware that it is within.

— Kahlil Gibran

Chapter 1

The Key to the Doorway

I have long felt compelled to write a book like this because I think that the subjects covered are crucial to our present-day nonmaterial needs. I hope this work can help to ready all of us for the changes in the Earth and in human consciousness that I think are approaching in the imminent future. In connection with this, it is my opinion that the vast majority of us are missing out on the most important element of our lives: at least an elemental knowledge of the invisible worlds that surround us and the invisible living entities who constantly interact with us. I am by no means an ultimate authority on the unseen realms, but I have at length researched, pondered and studied to the point where I believe I have a fair grasp of what goes on Out There. "Out There", or "Over There", are phrases used throughout this book. They are my terms for any realm that we cannot usually see or hear with our normal physical senses. I think there is not a more important thing we can do in this life than to try to find out why we are here—why—and to explore what it is that is Out There beyond the realm of our accepted level of reality.

I am going to touch on a lot of sensitive subjects, particularly in the first third of the book. I am going to touch on them, make my point and go on. Simple, brief and direct is my primary goal throughout the book. Frequently I will refer back to a subject already covered and perhaps expand on it even more at that point. I would have preferred to have made this book one continuous essay. But to make it a proper book, chapter-breaks had to be included. Hopefully the chapter interruption has not affected the continuity of the book.

We are, without doubt, surrounded by nonphysical beings that can see us while we, as a rule, cannot see them. I think these beings absolutely marvel at how willfully ignorant we are of our own immediate cosmic neighborhood. We are ignorant because we as a species generally haven't tried to understand this neighborhood. We haven't really looked. We have been so preoccupied with the pursuits of the physical—money, "security needs," food, sex and the multitude of other demanding distractions of the physical—that we have, as a result, generally ignored the ever-present nonphysical worlds.

I am sure that we are born into this world as sophisticated spiritual beings. But the physical body is like a hungry wild animal with its desires, demands, fears, hates, jealousies and so forth. As a result we have generally ignored our basic spiritual needs. Our success here on Earth is no doubt assessed by how well we master and control the demands and preoccupations of the physical body. It seems evident that somewhere along the line we have developed a limiting and debilitating tunnel vision which excludes that which we cannot hold in our hands.

What is perhaps worse is that we have developed, as a species, a general belief system that other worlds and entities don't even exist. Much of this denial has been imposed on us by organized religion. We have reverse-evolved, moving backwards from what should be by now our natural, quite advanced psychic awareness. We are, I think, living up to only 10% or less of our creative psychic potential. Modern scientific estimates say that we are using only 2.5% of our brains' abilities. The other 97.5% is lying dormant. For what? What is that other 97.5% intended for? That 97.5% is surely our key to the doorway of what we think of as the unknown. We call it unknown because we have neglected to acknowledge and open to this foreboding, fearful world and to use our psychic (or extrasensory) abilities in a useful, every-day, practical manner which would have long ago eliminated many of our primal fears.

Peoples we consider primitive, such as the non-city Aborigines, have fully developed their natural psychic/extrasensory, spiritual and self-healing potential. They have little money or possessions but in matters of essential evolution they are leagues ahead of us. It's interesting that many of the Aboriginal tribes of the remote outback have an attitude of disdain, even outright repulsion, toward "civilized" man. One member of a remote tribe who has had only rare contact with modern civilization had an interesting comment. He said that most civilized men and women are already dead; they just haven't been buried yet. It's something to think about.

Channels and mystics tell us that we have been asleep for a long time and it is now high time for us to wake up. Waking up may be simply a matter of turning our attention to the invisible unknown without fear. Then the portals to that unknown will reopen, causing and allowing an incredible upward transformation of all desirable aspects of humankind. It's not a particularly difficult or spiritual task; in fact, I believe it's a reasonably simple, practical process to access these realms. But we must believe or at least entertain the possibility that these realms are real and accessible before the door to the unknown will reopen on a large scale.

Am I tossing out here more useless opinions and theories among a million vague and unverifiable speculations already floating about? I have, myself, plowed through about a half million often ludicrous speculations from just about every printed and unprinted source imaginable. It's a confusing search and it causes one, at times, to want to turn away from all of it. Who is right and who is wrong? Who is deliberately lying and who, or what, is telling ironclad truth we must hear? Who is telling us in sugarcoated terms what we want to hear, for profit (theirs)? I've wanted to toss in the towel out of frustration innumerable times. But something unnameable drives me relentlessly to find satisfactory answers. The baying hound of truth won't leave me alone, day or night. If I turn away from it, the hound pursues me until I turn back to the arena and continue on with a sometimes infuriatingly frustrating search.

I think I have found some true answers and I want to share them with you. Why? Because I really think we have, on Earth, little time left. Perhaps years, perhaps months. Upcoming events will effect a profound change in human existence. A cleansing in all its ramifications is coming, be it catastrophic, economic, spiritual or alien—or all four. An understanding of the unseen realms will help us to endure and prosper in the challenges of the near future. Instead of going in blind, hopefully many of us will have our eyes and minds open and receptive, ready for a new chapter in human and Earth evolution. The ones, I think, who have their eyes and minds closed because of ignorance and choice are going to have an unnecessarily hard time of it. We shall see.

What exactly will the change be? I am quite certain it will be economic in the beginning, followed by a natural catastrophe along with nearly simultaneous spiritual and alien intervention. It will be a negative and fearful experience for those who choose to ignore the accelerating signs, warnings and obvious developments. Just two examples of this are, one, the U.S. economy is on the verge of total collapse because of a runaway national debt and two, Earthquake activity around the world has increased one hundred fold in the last ten years.

I have seen some of these invisible realms and entities I alluded to earlier. I have talked, in a fashion, to invisible beings in other places and worlds and dimensions. (More on this later.) My positive experiences with the realms of the invisible spur me on with even a greater enthusiasm to share with others what I have come to know as truth, or reality. None of this has to do with religion, religious doctrine or a religious viewpoint. I am not and never have been a religious person. I am, however, in the (new) classic sense a deeply spiritual person. I include that note to make it clear that I am not presenting this book from any sort of dogmatic, brainwashed or conditioned viewpoint. I consider myself a free-thinker. I am a nonconformist, and at times that has been costly.

It has been only in the past few years that I have been able to talk openly about some of what would probably be termed supernatural experiences that I have had, those experiences that involve only the invisible realms. For a long time I had a repressive fear of ridicule and humiliation if I talked openly of the highly out-of-the-normal situations with which I have been involved. Before this book is finished I am going to tell you how to personally experience these unseen realms too, not just distantly read about them. Much of what I have written about since my entry into this arena of the unseen goes smack against the grain of established social reality. The "reality" that we have shored up over the past thousands of years may be, and probably is, far from the reality we should be experiencing in an everyday manner. I think we got off the right road somewhere and got sidetracked or lost a long time ago. Along with hard-core religion, I think we can focus part of the blame on the unnatural development of a money system and the bankers who happily made it mandatory that dependence on money become the central motivation of all our lives. If we didn't have or need money, we would have less reason to fight among ourselves. Money, or the pursuit of things is the reason for 99% of our wars and person-to-person conflicts. Some might interpret the previous sentence as a struggle for power and control.

In an unseen sense I think the most important realm to us, the living, is that of the "dead"—or in other words, where we end up when our physical bodies die: the afterlife, Heaven, the other side, Valhalla , utopia, whatever the term. I think a basic knowledge of that level will benefit us all here and now. I have devoted a sizeable portion of this book to that subject. Every one of us, wherever we are, is here now for a reason, a purpose based on an agreement certainly established before we incarnated into this present life. No matter how good or bad our lives are, somehow it was planned for us that way or allocated to us so that we would learn something specific. Some people have extraordinarily difficult lives, as we all well know. If those burdened individuals can muster their physical and mental stamina and meet and beat those challenges (that is, see them for the lessons they are), they emerge unshakably strong. They win the battle, the test. The reward for meeting and beating these imposed or agreed-upon challenges is, I am sure, complete in an evolutionary sense. Unfortunately, if the particular life situation beats those people and they give up, they will have to confront the same things again here or in another place.

It's said that the Earth existence is condensed learning and can't be done the same way anywhere else. Because we are for a specified time physical beings, we immediately see or feel the results of our actions here on Earth, whether they be "good" or "bad." Everyone of us has had an agonizingly painful event and we would give anything to go back in time to replay it and do it differently. If it was a bad experience it probably hurts, and if we are intelligent and open-minded we wouldn't do the same thing over and over. Hopefully. But some people never learn. They repeat the same error or errors endlessly merely because they won't take a long, serious look at the situation and change it. If they reach the end of their lives and have learned little, they have to relive that stream of life again somewhere. It might be as a male the next time or as a female, perhaps in another place, but they will probably find themselves back on Earth with the same difficult situation to deal with until the situation is mastered or resolved. I think the reason, or at least surely one of the reasons, for our being physical here on Earth is to ultimately learn and earn unwaveringly ethical responsibility toward ourselves and all things. If we get kicked around or kick ourselves around enough and through sheer determination gain control of our particular situation, mastering our emotions and physical needs and greed and addictive desire, we become stable and responsible individuals worthy of unlimited cosmic power.

Over There our power of creation and destruction is probably near absolute, or at least at higher levels. We no doubt (I hope) asked for this condensed, sometimes intensely painful learning experience and to be physical on Earth so that we would progress further Over There. Otherwise, Over There a lot of us would be little more than unstable, irresponsible adolescents possessing limitless power — a child in a universal dynamite factory playing with a cigarette lighter. Knowing how violent some people are down here we do not find it hard to visualize the consequences if they were Over There and not responsible for unlimited power. Once we have mastered our assigned lessons here, we are undoubtedly then worthy of unlimited power Over There. They of the high realms then can trust us with power; we will create with it and not destroy with it. Look around at some of the people you know who instead of living conscientiously hurt and destroy everything in their path with little or no conscience or remorse. Those types have a long way to go. No one Over There is going to hand them unlimited power. It doesn't matter what people do for a living or how much money they make. Position in life is not particularly pertinent. Poor people get the same opportunities as rich people, maybe more, because poor people often have few comforts and little security.

We have all done things in our lives that give us a cold, guilt-ridden, sinking feeling in the stomach when we recollect the event. If whatever it was was an accident, an honest accident, I think it is all right. But if the "accident" was intentional and planned and somebody got hurt and hurt badly physically or emotionally, I think the event has to be looked at with careful introspection, looked at carefully, so it is thoroughly understood, picked apart feeling by feeling, moment by moment; then honest effort made to not do the same thing again. We can learn from the experience in a positive way.

Karma? Someone we were involved with got hurt in some way, perhaps very badly, perhaps even killed, and we are thinking that according to the law of karma that person, in retribution, is going to get even and do the same sort of thing to us in the next lifetime. I firmly believe that karma is a falsehood, as are so many other of the irrational, basically unfounded and created fears that have controlled us for so long, fears usually derived from some religion or religious figure who long ago was in a position of personal power and profit. The myth was anchored and it lived and lives in humankind's consciousness, unchallenged until now when so many are questioning all past beliefs. Do I think karma exists? My answer would be yes and no. Yes if we believe it and no if we don't. If we think someone is going to exact revenge on us because of something we've done, we will create or find a situation in which something correspondingly will indeed happen to us. So in that sense, karma is real. But if our goal is to be a good person, if we don't really believe in karma, if we carefully learn in a good way from a bad experience and try not to do that same thing again (or let it happen again), karma does not exist. I am certain of it. Although I know I am stepping on hallowed ground here—this would preclude even strong past-life beliefs in karma . Say, for example, that in this lifetime and the ten before that we firmly believed in karmic retribution for our actions. Complete nonbelief in karma now will, I am sure, cancel karmic debts we think we may owe. But this does not include contracts or agreements made in another place or lifetime with another person or persons. Contracts and agreements are far beyond the scope of this book and individuals will have to research this possibility on their own.

I've read in some of the books of Eastern philosophy that we have an incredible number of lifetimes in the Earth embodiment. Some of these much read books claim that we have hundreds, thousands or even hundreds of thousands of lifetimes here. I hope not. Speaking for myself, at least, I am going to do the best I can to get it completed this time and I am not coming back. If they try to send me back here they are going to get one doozy of an argument. I know that there is something Out There that is infinitely better than what we have here, I've seen it, and that is where I want to be! Perhaps what I say here will help to get us all Over There to stay—where we belong.

Unseen Beings, Unseen Worlds

...they forget that, with all their own admirable progress in material invention, with all the far-reaching data of their acquired science, with all the vast extent of their commercial and economic conquests, they themselves have ceased to be natural.

— W.Y. Evans Wentz,
speaking on the subject of
civilized man — in 1911

Chapter 2

A Chorus of Voices in the Distance

I think I have read or am aware of just about every paranormal, esoteric, spiritual, and metaphysical book in print and many that are out of print. In part, as a consensus of that reading and other research, I think our total lifetimes here on Earth number fewer than one hundred. Fast learners probably do it in as few as a half dozen lifetimes. Intelligence and money have little to do with it. Desire and curiosity have everything to do with it. If you want, you will.

I haven't mentioned love yet. Isn't love the key to it all? I think so. The key to it all must be love and kindness. How we feel about ourselves and the Earth and its living creations is the foundation. If we can love all things and people as brothers and sisters, with a gentle Christ-like quality, that is, I am sure, the spring-board to a fine and proper position on the Other Side.

The last paragraph illustrates one of my own greatest challenges. I am probably one of the easiest people on Earth to get along with, and I love good, real and honest people who are conscientious. If people treat me fairly I will do anything for them. But there have been a few folks I have trusted who have, intentionally and with planning, done something to me so reprehensible that if they had continued with it or had done it again, I might have taken enormous pleasure in strangling them slowly. The best I can do in these situations is, upon recognition, avoid these types of predatory/destructive people and steer around them. I often remind myself of the age-old saying, "the fool stays and fights and the wise man walks away." It's not easy. It took me forty years of my life to deduce that this world is well-stocked with people who would, given the chance, manipulate, control and destroy another person in a moment and not have a shred of remorse or guilt about it. This is mostly derived from not acknowledging their own personal failures but instead blaming others for their own failures, often harshly. I used to trust everyone completely. I grew up in rural New England where a handshake was enough. A man's word was his word and it could be depended on without lawyers or contracts. But out in the modern, real world I have discovered that that doesn't usually work very well. I have learned the hard way to be selective and cautious. Some of us learn things a little slower than others. I do however have a method of dealing with fierce and manipulative personality types, or others. I visualize them surrounded with beautiful and fragrant white flowers, such as lilies of the valley, white roses or orchids. Then I can deal rationally with that person. Try it sometime.

In my metaphysical travels I have encountered a number of people, men and women, who seem to know everything about everything. In the field of spirituality, UFOs, aliens, esoteric studies, or just about any other subject they have a cut-and-dried answer. The only answer. I avoid these people like the plague. These people often have a bad case of NABS—New Age Bullshit. Unfortunately, they usually find enough willing listeners to keep them in business, to the detriment of the willing listener. I have found that if someone claims to know everything, in reality they usually know nothing. There is a great difference between real wisdom and imagined wisdom. I have noticed over and over that those who possess real wisdom and knowledge often speak very little and usually offer their advice or opinion only after being asked. Some time ago I developed a motto for myself: *Question Everything*. I could include with this *Never, Ever, Assume Anything*. I don't mean shut down to everything. What I mean is to not be gullible and to maintain a healthy and intelligent skepticism toward just about everything. Be a free thinker and make well-grounded decisions, especially in the realm of the new spirituality and the paranormal.

In the past half dozen years or so I have developed an analytical interest in a subject that is generally avoided as a topic of discussion in modern society. It is death and dying. There is often a great deal of fear or denial associated with the topic of death and dying. From my own experience a close, fearless look at the death scenario resulted in the terror aspect falling away like dust in the wind. The death experience should be understood, not at all feared. As I have explained in my other books and several of my magazine articles, I am one who has a relentless, rather reckless at times, curiosity. I want to know what is going on. I want to know what gives something its substance, no matter how sensitive the subject might be. Death is no exception. I have found that as I have gone deeply into exploring the subject of death, the fear-and-loathing factor was gradually replaced with one of utter fascination. Most of us have turned away from thinking creatively about the death experience because of the fear-based unknowns that go along with it. I am not talking here about conditions that lead up to the death experience but about the final experience itself. We die and then what, what happens after that? My interest lies in this aspect. One of the things that I have more than confirmed to my satisfaction is that we certainly do live on after physical death and that we are not physical beings for long. This Earth experience is just a stopover. There is plenty of proof of this. Our natural, permanent state of being is not physical but that of a being of pure energy—of light, if you will. I might add that I don't think there is any difference between light and energy in a spiritual sense. I think they are one and the same.

Right at the point of death and shortly thereafter is when things get interesting. That's when we return to our real home. Getting re-oriented to our real home Over There can be an unsettling experience for those who think being physical is all there is or for those who have indeed forgotten on some level that they are, in reality, not physical beings but beings of light or pure energy. I think if we can all learn all we can about the dying experience and what happens immediately afterwards, then we will be in a much better position to learn and gain from the Earth/death experience while on the journey back to our origin. Most of us go into dying confused, unprepared, fearful and uninformed, not a good way to do it. When I cash in the chips I want to be as ready for the trip as I can be. Maybe I can help a few people to prepare for it as well, with little fear and a measure of pre-knowledge. Due to the experiences of so many Earth humans in the past who have died and returned temporarily to their bodies to tell of what they have seen and learned, we now know much about the seemingly mysterious afterlife, especially through the research of authors like Elizabeth Kubler Ross and Raymond Moody.

At this point, I want to interject the subject of suicide. Mention the topic of suicide in an open discussion and see how fast someone changes the subject. No one, it seems, wants to discuss suicide. I have done a large measure of clinical thinking, talking and reading on the matter. Here is what I have concluded: Anyone who is seriously contemplating suicide shouldn't do it! If we can talk another person out of it we should. If someone has already committed suicide or will do it no matter what anyone says, then that's the way it is. The problem with suicide is that we are not completing our life's agreement or assignment. I know the pain and suffering some people go through. I've seen plenty of it—haven't we all—but that suffering is part of that person's pre-set life experience and the experience must be followed to a natural conclusion. (Intelligent and conscientious free will can indeed override and change anything, but few people exercise their right of creative free will.) I don't for a second envy any of those people, and I'm glad I'm not in a position of constant suffering and pain. If we do terminate our physical existence, we are, I am now sure, immediately reincarnated into another body somewhere and we are going to have to face the exact conditions we sought to avoid in the previous life. This scenario will continue until we master that particular life situation. Nobody said physical life would be easy but I am certain the rewards are great upon the successful completion of it. I am quite sure that in past lives I have suicided at least a half dozen times, so on a deep level I think I have an innate knowing of the experience and the "penalties."

A note: Today is September 21, 1993. A few hours ago, at 9:30 a.m., while doing a final rewrite of this short section on suicide, I got an urgent message to call a friend who lives in the Midwest. When I began speaking to my friend on the phone I knew psychically that there had been a sudden, recent, and extremely violent death near him.

As it turned out, a member of his family, an eighteen-year-old boy, had, at 4:30 p.m. the afternoon before, gone to visit his girlfriend at the farm where she lived. The boy was also from a farm family. She told him then that their relationship was over and gave him back his ring. He already knew that she had been seeing other boys. The boy, who had just entered college, went out to his pickup truck and shot himself to death with a rifle. The call from my friend came exactly at the time when I was working on the suicide section. Coincidence and the universe do indeed work in mysterious ways. I don't normally get calls like this, so I'm sure there is some sort of message in it for all of us. I'm not exactly sure what the message is, except that perhaps it emphasizes and underlines what I have written about suicide.

The boy's parents had had a dramatic close sighting of three triangular, pulsing UFOs just prior to the boy's death. A connection?

Getting back to the natural death experience: There are a number of situations which I now know to be rather evident. Let's take an average scenario. Most people die in hospitals or at home in bed. A typical death is one in which a person who is of advanced years has gone through some sort of illness or regressive infirmity. Relatives are gathered around the death bed waiting for the final moment. In some rare cases his or her face suddenly brightens and he beams with great joy. He says something like, "The light, the light! It is so beautiful! It (or they) are here for me!" Or he says something such as, "It's June (his long-dead wife)! She has come for me, she is holding out her hand to me!" At that point he or she leaves the physical body. But many people, probably the majority, pass on quickly and don't have these visual pre-death visitation experiences. Some who have died in accidents or elsewhere and returned have said they found themselves floating above the car accident or whatever and were looking down on their own dead body. It was as if they were observing a movie. Interestingly, there is seldom any grief involved in looking down at one's own lifeless body. Most departees are relieved and glad to be done with it all, to be free of what they said was a cumbersome and restricting physical experience.

A variety of things can transpire from here — such as at the point of departure from the physical body a sun-bright white light may be seen or a beloved friend or perhaps a relative may be recognized coming toward them to take them "home." I was reading a few years ago the story of a man who had been regressed hypnotically and recalled under hypnosis being killed in the Civil War. It was close to the end of the war and his Confederate detachment was out of food and ammunition. The Confederates were crossing a wide, shallow creek when Union troops hidden in the trees opened fire on them. They were caught in the middle of the open creek and all of them were either shot or bayonetted. Most of the unfortunate Confederates lived in the same local area of the same state. The man, under hypnosis, saw himself getting to his feet and looking down at his own body floating face down in the creek. He realized then that he was dead. He looked around, and the other Confederate soldiers were also standing and quietly looking confused and forlornly down at their dead physical bodies drifting in the creek. It was at that point that an old man dressed like a farmer appeared in their midst. He was recognized by the men as a fellow countryman who had died years before. The old man was, like a grandfather, loved and respected by the country folk, the dead Confederates who knew him. The old man said to them in a quiet tone, "Come along, boys. The war's over for you." They all went with the old farmer, but under hypnosis the man could not recall where they went or

A Chorus of Voices in the Distance

were taken. This is often the case in hypnosis past life or otherwise. For some reason the memory of what is beyond is usually blocked or inaccessible.

Here is where it all gets really interesting. As I mentioned a lot of different things can occur at this point, which is all the more reason to have as much knowledge as reasonably possible of the death experience. The "dead" person who is now out of his or her physical body may encounter a number of situations.

In some cases they return to their physical bodies immediately because their life experiences have not been completed; they may be asked to go back or may simply be sent back to Earth by a higher power. Quite often these returnees have vivid memories of the out-of-body experience and they often bring back a clear glimpse of the Great Beyond. Some returnees, like ex-CIA agent Dannion Brinkley, write extraordinary books about it. Most say the experience of being on the other side was so beautiful and wonderful that they can hardly wait to return to the other side, no matter what reason compelled them back into their Earth bodies. Usually the reason for the Earth return is some sort of family obligation or some kind of responsibility that could not be left unfinished.

Sometimes recently dead people may absolutely refuse to believe that they are dead and become anchored, or trapped, for a time on the Earth plane. These people may wander aimlessly for many, many years (years in our time frame, anyway; it may be hours in their time frame) amongst us, the living (this is the realm of the "ghost"), until at some point they realize or are finally convinced that they are really dead and can go into the light or on to their proper level. These people without physical bodies can be, but are usually not, a problem to us. I'll talk more about this later and show you why they can be a problem—a big one.

Newly deceased people, while they are standing there wondering what happened or where they are, may begin to hear softly tinkling bells or chimes or the beautiful soft singing of a chorus of many voices somewhere in the distance. Along with the chimes and singing, a small at first, but blindingly bright white light may appear and gently and lovingly beckon the person toward it. This light has an attraction that usually is irresistible. But, people who have just gone through the death experience may actually be frightened by the light because they refuse to believe they are dead and they may actually and literally run from the light. They hide from the light. The light never pursues them. The ones who run from the light, it seems, often have a rigid belief that Hell exists and that they will end up in Hell if they go to and into the light. Guilt about something they did while alive is often the motive. And then there are those who are so addicted to Earth living they simply refuse to go on. However, most people are willingly and magnetically drawn into the light. It feels incredibly loving, vibrant, alive and comforting. As these willing people draw closer to the light they quickly become accustomed to the blazing brightness, feel the love and merge into the light. The ones who have come back, temporarily, from this light experience can scarcely find the words to describe the compassion and beauty they have encountered. As they first enter the light they begin to experience a sensation of gradual acceleration and rapidly increasing speed. Ones who remember usually describe having been in some sort of tunnel and the feeling of fantastic speed and going a vast distance is acute. They sometimes give an account of traveling through a gray zone first, and an extremely unpleasant sensation is always associated with this zone, a place, it seems, that is relatively close to the Earth plane, meaning us. It may actually and literally be in our own Earth atmosphere. As the sensation of speed reaches its peak, most participants describe passing through numerous layers or levels (which often have colors) until after a short time they see the end of the tunnel. An even brighter light is at that point apparent at the end of the tunnel.

Finally, the travelers emerge out of the tunnel. They then might experience any of a large variety of situations. Upon emerging from the tunnel people might, to their utter joy, meet "deceased" beloved family or friends. It may be one individual or it may be as many as a dozen or more, but they are always those who were very dear to the newly dead person. The setting of such a meeting is always a beautiful place, perhaps a crystalline city or a magnificent meadow or forest. The colors of the plants, flowers, trees, sky or whatever is

A Chorus of Voices in the Distance

there are nothing like we have on Earth. Returnees always have groping difficulty finding any words to describe the splendor, the glory, the majesty, the love and the comfort they felt while Over There. Often, an orb of bright light will be waiting at the end of the tunnel. It takes a few moments for people to realize that the light is actually a living being.

All who have returned say that human physical eyes could never behold such a light. In a matter of minutes the dead beings adjust to this light and see that the light has within it the shape of a human form, although the form is made up of pure light of a single color or of many colors. These beings of light may be of any color of the spectrum but it seems that they most often vibrate at a color of white, gold or silver. That light is, in some instances, discovered to be a living, higher, "future" aspect of the dead person himself or herself. Or, as in many cases, the person in that shroud of light may be a beloved former acquaintance or (long dead) relative.

It seems, in addition, that very highly evolved spirits often choose, or chose, to live on Earth as everyday, ordinary people such as librarians, maids, bus drivers, carpenters or housewives. We might think that they would incarnate in an easy life as people in an exalted position of fame, money or power, but it's evident that they are frequently more interested in the everyday happenstances of everyday people. It may be this type of person who is the greeter. For example, deceased Uncle Bill, who was a taxi cab driver for 47 years while on Earth, turns out to be a tremendously advanced being Over There.

The "dead" people newly emerged from the tunnel may then be taken by whomever meets them on a guided tour of dimensions, universes, star systems, great crystalline cities of light or even magnificent ethereal, forests. They may be taken to meet Great Ones, the ones of ancient, universal wisdom who were, in most instances, associates of those newly arrived persons somewhere during some chapter of that newly arrived person's Earth's evolution.

One aspect that is always encountered is that new arrivals on the other side are shown, as though they were watching a movie, their most recent life on Earth from beginning to end. This is one part that I am working on. I am going to be ready for this and so should we all. No one Over There ever judges any newly arrived person for their "sins." They don't judge us; Over There, we judge ourselves. Are you ready? In this realm of spirit there is only gentle, loving acceptance of people, no matter how well or badly they conducted themselves on the Earth plane. The new arrivals are shown every day-to-day detail and thought of their lives, and it can be sheer agony for some of them, especially when they see the missed opportunities for spiritual advancement and growth during the last life. They see what they did in a loving way and the ramifications of that love as it spreads from the initial act or acts of love and kindness. They also see and feel what they did to themselves and others in a harmful, hateful way, and then they watch what those people, in turn, did to another person in revenge, and on and on. Love spreads. Hate spreads. It quickly becomes obvious that one of our greatest lessons is to learn love, tolerance, forgiveness, helpfulness and gentleness toward ourselves, others and things of the Earth. Gaining knowledge is surely important but love and kindness seem to be the determining factors. There are great rewards Over There for what we personally do here in regard to all the positive aspects of love. Those who maintained love, patience and understanding in their lives, especially under conditions of grinding adversity, I believe *always* go to high levels of spirituality. Those who have intentionally focused on anger, jealousy, hate and greed and revenge in a quest for ego-power over people often go or get stuck on a lower level of what I see as ten or so levels. In a short time these negatively based people are reincarnated back into the Earth system to eventually, by trial and error, learn through love instead of through hate, ego and destructive power; or they may be sent to a different life-experiencing location that is not at all human.

The last situation people might encounter right after death would be to *immediately* find themselves traveling through the tunnel toward the light at the end of the tunnel and to whatever awaits them at the next step.

These generalizations are the only ones I am aware of through first hand experience and research but there certainly may be more and there may be many more variations of each one that I mentioned. It won't be long before we will develop a technology that will enable us to actually talk in person, to those on the Other Side, like ringing someone up on the phone. Some scientific researchers are very close to perfecting that technology now. Then we will, I hope, at that point of direct link-up resolve 2000-plus years of mass confusion. To be here to watch this recentering activity would be greatly interesting to me. Someone, you can be sure, somewhere along the line will try to regulate it and cash in on it. You know, Dial-A-Ghost, 1-900-111-GHOST, $10 a minute.

Unseen Beings, Unseen Worlds

ECLECTIC: "Selecting what appears to be best or true in various and diverse doctrines or methods; rejecting a single, unitary, and exclusive interpretation, doctrine or method."

Chapter 3

The Astral Plane

The astral and in particular the lowest astral planes have always held a measure of fascination for me because of a big "why." Why? Where is it? Why is it? My conclusion is that I don't want to go there. I wouldn't want anyone to go there, and a bit of forewarning and knowledge are probably the keys to staying out of the place. Gathering realistic information about the astral hasn't been easy. Evidently, people who find themselves in the lower astral, or in the gray zone, and who stay there, usually by choice, do so largely of their own accord out of fear of what they did on the Earth plane in a physical addictive negative sense and out of a fear that they would end up in Hell. Little do they realize that they are in Hell already.

Whether they do or don't realize that they are now dead, evidently the fear of a perceived Hell is a deciding factor for most in their predicament in the astral, and it is the reason most stay there. Does Hell exist? It does—in the minds of the people who create it, no matter who they are or where they are. Yet another closet monster that we have organized religion and others to thank for. Hell, I think, in the usually assumed religious sense of the term, is located in the lowest astral realms. Hell is not, in a literal sense, real. I surmise that those endeared folk heroes, Satan and Lucifer, are real, living entities who are operating from the astral realm and are doing so with the full knowledge and allowance of the Creator Force. If so, what is Satan and Lucifer's point of origin? Where did they come from? Are they or were they fallen angels? Who knows? Does it matter? Nothing is more powerful than the Creator Force. If something "evil" exists it does so because a higher power allows it to exist as a teaching tool. We don't have to participate in that "evil," Satan or otherwise, unless we want to. It is a choice of good or bad, love or hate, creation or destruction. Several choices with infinite variations in between.

Something Wicked This Way Comes

I want to talk here about one of my all time favorite subjects. It is that of the (... long big drum roll) "Dark Forces." I believe that the popular idea of a malevolent dark force that is well-organized and massed and is systematically trying to destroy us, mind and body, is total, complete, absolute rubbish. I like to think I know what I am talking about because I have seen a lot of dark force crap (probably too much) over the years. A lot of people, as in a melodramatic soap opera, like to get into the spine-chilling drama of a mythical, all powerful invisible dark force trying to impose something on them or take something away from them. It, in that form, does not exist.

Dark forces, in the generally accepted meaning of the term, are manufactured through the paranoia of the mass consciousness of much of humankind. Dark forces, the dark, the dark side and so on have been invented by mankind and have been given fearful false power over mankind. Ask any Christian about demons and one is likely to get a comprehensive scare-em-good rundown on the subject. In knowledge there is power. If we can rationally understand something, we can confront it and, if we wish, eliminate it. I have known individuals who have started dark force rumors and those rumors, if conditions were right, anchored and spread in receptive and susceptible minds like dark age witch hunts. It has been a long time since the Salem Witch Trials but things are no different now. When I first moved to Sedona seven years ago, I was at the time channeling a rather futuristic and controversial, anything-but-negative entity named Kaal and because of that controversy someone started a rumor that I was working for and with the dark forces; the rumor caught on. If it hadn't been for a few influential local New-Agers going around and impressing upon certain people that the whole thing had gone way too far and it had to stop immediately, I might have stayed here only a short time. A very short time. Small minds often do small and petty things, men and women anywhere. I will say this several times in the book: Love yourself, be happy with who you are, know who you are, trust in Spirit and in your own power and you will *never* have to concern yourself with any kind of a negative entity on or from any level of existence. For a human there is an inviolate, universal power in that state of being and awareness.

If you believe in advancing Dark Forces, then they are and will be real. We have enough real problems without creating false problems. There is no doubt we do have "enemies" out there and I hope I can make a separation, a differentiation between them and the imposing notion of mythical dark forces. There are astrals we need to deal with and there are several groups of ETs we need to deal with but these are real, tangible entities we must understand, categorize and deal with logically and rationally. This is *not* a situation that is in any way out of our control. I think we have far more to be concerned about from the treachery of some of our fellow human beings (the real origin of the dark force?) than we ever would from any kind of ethereal and unseen Dark Force.

To consider another aspect of the lower astral, let's go back now to the dead fellow who has just crossed over and who out of fear runs and hides from the light. Sometimes those who have left their physical bodies but remain on the Earth plane stay here among us with the same physical appearance they had before they died. This static condition can exist for as long as they want it to be that way when instead they could have gone on into higher realms and gotten the help or opportunities they needed. Evidently, in most cases of this kind a guide, a teacher, a former Earth relative or some other being will come back to try to persuade the recalcitrant or refusing dead person to come along with him or her into the light through the tunnel, the portal. But still, some people might refuse to believe that they are dead: they may have an overpowering Earth addiction, fear and/or conviction that they are going to end up in Hell or perhaps be punished for some evil deed they have done. These confused people can indeed wander among us for several years or even hundreds of years. I have "seen" some of these people. I have mentally and telepathically talked with great accuracy to some of them. (We all can; it's not particularly difficult. I'll get to that later.) These "ghosts" can see us as plainly as you and I can see each other. However, as a rule, we cannot see them. Olaf Johnsson, who was one of the world's all-time greatest psychics, said that not all ghosts among us are living astral beings but are often merely energy shadows of a person who had died. These shadows can remain and can move about of their own accord long after the shadow's owner has left and gone on. Eventually, after a number of years, these "shadows" simply discharge or dissipate. I agree with Johnsson completely on this because some ghosts I have encountered seem to have no life essence whatever and seem to be unaware of attempts to communicate with them. In a similar but opposite vein, some Earth-bound "live" astrals can be extremely dangerous to us—but not if we know about them. Somehow the simple awareness of their existence on our part keeps the bad ones, the predators, from negatively influencing us.

I have proven to myself that this Awareness-of-Them procedure works. On a number of occasions I have worked with people thousands of miles away who seemed to have had a valid astral problem. At the point where they resolved that the astral would no longer bother them the problem vanished. Here is why low astrals can be dangerous to us. We have all heard of possession, it's real. I've seen three authentic cases of it close up, first hand. I actually watched once as a woman came under possession by an unseen entity. (I'll go into that in a few pages.)

Some people who no longer have a physical body but who have

remained among us here on the Earth plane for some reason I don't fully understand can in some circumstances enter a physical body (us) and at times overpower us and become the dominant personality. Psychologist Edith Fiore in her excellent book *The Unquiet Dead*, theorizes from a well-researched clinical standpoint that schizophrenia and multiple personality disorder are in reality (in most cases) situations in which a person is possessed by a discarnate human or in some cases, many astral humans. I think the most extreme known case of multiple possession is one in which twenty discarnate astrals were controlling one Earth human. If astrals were, in their lives on Earth, destructive people, they are no different in most cases once they end up on the astral plane. If a person was a particularly evil person here, a rapist, a murderer or manipulator or had a severe addiction to drugs or alcohol or sex etc., that person usually retains those same traits on the lower levels of the astral. As the old saying among psychics goes, if they were a bastard here chances are they are still a bastard Over There. Old habits die hard. We don't automatically turn into angels the moment we cross over.

I think there are two basic levels to the lower astral. I will simply call them one and two. At this point, to reiterate, there are probably ten levels immediately available to us after we die. Level ten would be the highest spiritual level we can attain from here. There may be, and probably are, a hundred more after that I don't know; I can't even guess. Level one would be the level that dead persons remain on who continue to stay on the Earth plane with us. Two, I am sure, is what has generally come to be known as the "gray zone." I have never been able to grasp any real kind of firm definition or understanding about the gray zone except that it is a heinously horrible place. A fair definition might be that it is where one is purged, as in the Catholic's religious definition of purgatory. It is evidently a reserved place where intentionally negative and destructive former Earth humans get the chance to act out the worst of negative human traits on each other until they are sick and tired of the pain, suffering and repitition and ask or plead for help in getting out of the gray zone. It seems they have to be sick enough of the place to desperately want out and to sincerely want to change their old ways.

have a genuine desire they are taken out of the grey zone by
r being and go to a level of spirituality where they can heal and learn. That is another one of the reasons I am doing all I can to learn as much as I can about the "hereafter." I don't want to have *anything* to do with the gray zone (I've had psychic glimpses of it) and hopefully neither should you, now or ever. The place is a nightmare.

It's evident that some astrals, both low and high levels, can focus enough energy to materialize back amongst us. Some asked (and ask) not to be touched but some have been hugged and/or had their hands held. For a few minutes they were physical humans again. Raymond Moody, Ph.D., has extraordinary books and articles on this subject. His books are available in any main stream or new age bookstore.

In this next aspect of the astral I am referring to a probable interdimensional intervention into our space by creatures from the unseen. These creatures seem somehow to be closely related to the human astral. This is no doubt in part where the fearful, human attacking incubus and succubus legends derive from. The incubus and succubus phenomenon is extraordinarily strange. These anything-but-human entities, at least some of them, may come from a bizarre dimension or level which we have little knowledge of. It's fortunate that attacks from these "creatures" are extremely rare. I have interviewed three people who I would consider to have had genuine contact with an incubus or a succubus.

The best defense against the gray zone incubus or succubus or anything that might be perceived as threatening or dangerous is to be aware of it and have a strong positive-minded desire to have nothing to do with it in any way. Knowledge is power. Ignorance is servitude. I have read that a powerful, advanced being of light will sometimes venture into the gray zone to rescue a curious higher spirit or out-of-body traveler who got too close and got pulled in. Not a fun place. There are lots of tales of the gray zone in hundreds of books, some a thousand or more years old.

I suspect that the famous Spanish painter Francisco de Goya (1746-1828) somehow through ignorance got himself snared by the inhabitants of the gray zone. His paintings, now priceless, went from bright, cheery and vibrantly colorful to dark, gloomy, dreary and drab with a nightmarish, deathlike quality to them. I had the opportunity to closely inspect one of Goya's huge originals in the Prado Museum in Madrid and it was one of the most ghoulish and feral depictions of primal human fear and emotion that I have ever seen. The Flemish Renaissance artist Hieronymus Bosch ("El Bosco") also depicted nightmarish scenes reminiscent of the lower astral zone.

Unseen Beings, Unseen Worlds

> "It will be hereafter proved that the human soul, even in this life, is in constant communication with the spiritual world, and that these are susceptive of mutual impressions. But ordinarily their impressions are unperceived by us."
>
> — Immanuel Kant

Chapter 4

The Light of the Creator Force

So we have those people who, after death, might have gone on to a higher level but instead stayed (for whatever reason) here amongst us. From research and personal experience I know this to be an absolutely real situation. The majority of the world population either doesn't know anything about astrals (or ghosts) or doesn't *want* to know anything about astrals. Denial, in general, is one of the greatest challenges that at present faces humanity as a race. I think denial on all levels has come to be humankind's major block to constructive advancement.

How we can guard or protect ourselves against astrals from the two lowest levels: One, knowledge again – we can be aware of the astral and the possibility of influence and possession and in our own power to not participate in negative influence. Two, we can request protection from High Spirit against influence from the astral. Three, we can visualize filling our bodies with blazing white light, packing our bodies with it and visualizing the white light moving from the center of the body and expanding out two or three feet, surrounding the body. We are then in a bubble of white light. It works. Either it is in actuality the white light of the Creator Force which low astrals cannot tolerate or it is an activation of the power of the subconscious to guard against or remedy a low astral influence or attack or both. Another possibility is that a powerful Spirit, because we have asked, watches over us, and an astral, seeing the Spirit's energy field close to us, beats a hasty retreat to a safer and more approachable human victim.

The following is another protection method that I feel is a very good one, although I feel the object, a bracelet, neck chain or waist-chain, could be dispensed with. I will always maintain that the real power is in the consciousness or subconsciousness, not in an object such as a crystal, etc. This is from the 28-page booklet, Psychic Self Defense, by Llewellyn Publications: "While psychic self-defense is just part of, a result of, a total program of *psychic well-being* that involves daily psychic exercises to channel spiritual energies and strengthen your aura, there is no reason that you should remain without psychic protection . . . *starting right now!*

"Take an object that you can wear or keep with you at all times. A ring or wristwatch will do, but a bracelet, necklace or waist-chain is better. Clean the chosen object in some way; the feeling that it is really clean should culminate what you've done. Seat yourself comfortably, preferably with your back straight, your feet together and the chosen object held loosely in your strongest hand.

"Close your eyes and physically relax your body. Breathe slowly and evenly. With each in-breath feel a flow of energy rise from your feet to the top of your head and with each out-breath feel that energy flow from the top of your head to your feet. Feel yourself calmly growing in strength as the energy flows through your body. After ten or more breaths, when you feel strong and alert, visualize a sphere of pure white light just above your head and know that this is your own Highest Self—free of all fear and pain, pure in the Divine Force that is everywhere.

"Visualize that sphere form an egg-shape of intense blue light all around you, and know that this is your psychic shield that will protect you from harm as it grows in strength. Continue breathing gently and evenly, feeling the strength in your body while holding this image. Grasp the chosen object tightly in your hand and feel that strength suddenly surge into your hand and into the object. Hold that object, hold that feeling, and hold the image of your psychic shield all around you. Project that fully charged battery, constantly energizing your psychic shield. *You are protected!*"

If a person has a sudden and dramatic 360-degree change in personality and character there is a fair possibility that that person may be being influenced and manipulated by a discarnate entity. An example would be a well balanced man who never drank, took drugs or was combative but who suddenly became a heavy drinker, recklessly took drugs and/or for no reason began abusing his wife, friends and associates. The possessing entity is acting out its previous human traits through a body that it can once again express itself through, however vicariously. So there is a pretty good possibility that anyone who has a sudden, violent shift in character and personality may be sick in a different way than is conventionally presumed. I have known people who had two distinct and opposing personalities. One personality was pleasant and passive and the other was vicious and aggressive, off and on, back and forth. Now, years later, I know that these people may well have been under possession by an astral entity.

I have never been able to understand to my satisfaction how some no-longer-physical beings can, when conditions are right, enter into and take over a living person's body. By living, I mean still physically here on the Earth. But a discarnate entity can completely control and dictate every facet of the life of a still-physical human. The evidence is there, plenty of it. There are many excellent, clinical type, books on the subject of possession.

I firmly believe the only reason possession can happen is that the vast majority of us are willfully and blindly unaware that a possible condition of possession can exist. This condition of possible possession has, no doubt, existed since mankind first appeared on this planet. If a person was mean, manipulative and vindictive in a recent past life, chances are he or she is still the same Over There, the only difference being the absence of a physical body. The implications of this for us who are still physical I hope are clear. The simple awareness of this possible condition of discarnate influence is, I believe, complete insurance that it will never happen to a physical Earth human. Cases of multiple personalities and schizophrenia may indeed not be diseases or disorders at all, but simply possession by a discarnate personality or a number of discarnate personalities.

Once I actually watched as a woman became overpowered, or possessed, by a discarnate personality.

In 1984, when I was living in northern California, I took a four-month workshop based on the book *The Teachings of the Inner Christ*, a superior work. The workshop was led by a woman who was a master of the teaching—I'll call her Ellen—and over time, the eighteen of us who had signed up and committed ourselves to taking the course from beginning to end became like a close-knit family.

The classes were being conducted at night in a large office building. One evening during the second month of the workshop, a woman who had a special evening appointment with a chiropractor in another part of the building came into our room. She was curious about what we were doing and asked politely if she could sit near the group circle and watch. What we did in the class was meditate, read chapters from the book and practice channeling, then discuss our experiences. Ellen, our group leader, replied that it was all right for the woman to watch and listen to what we were doing.

I am by habit an intently watchful and observant person. The woman visitor, I saw, was about thirty-five years old and pretty, with dark brown eyes and brown hair. She was about five feet six inches in height and was a bit overweight. The class went on. I kept glancing at the woman, whom I'll call Jan. I couldn't help but notice subtle ongoing changes in her posture and facial expressions.

About an hour before Jan had walked into the room we had all been discussing the sensation of a disturbingly negative unseen entity which we all had felt moving about the room. It had come, or been drawn, probably out of curiosity about what we were doing. Out of the corner of my eye I had watched a massive, fog-like blackness moving in the far right corner of the room and I had mentioned it to the class. We weren't particularly concerned about the intruder because we always performed a ritual meditation calling on High Spirit for protection. We also did white light cleansing and protection exercises at the beginning of each class. It never once crossed any of our minds that the woman sitting in, Jan, might be in any sort of jeopardy or danger. But that, as we were going to see, was about to change.

I was observing the visiting woman with mounting concern. If I ever see again what I saw happening then, I will, if I can, stop it in a second. But it was not my class, not my group, although I have conducted many of my own varied classes before and since. Ellen, who had had many years of previous experience as a class leader, was also carefully watching the same changes in our visitor.

Keep in mind that the visiting woman, Jan, knew nothing about what was going on and was simply waiting quietly to be called in for her chiropractic appointment. There was no way she could have been conditioned to expect anything, usual or unusual.

I was growing more and more uneasy by the moment because of what I was watching and I wondered why Ellen didn't do something. But she did nothing. Whether it was out of fear, ignorance or curiosity, I'll never know. In the beginning, we in the group had agreed, at Ellen's insistence, that she was to be the complete leader, the control of the group, with no competition from us. She was a compassionate, but strong-willed and decisive woman.

Over a period of twenty minutes, Jan went from a patient, serene, relaxed and softly smiling lady waiting to be called in for her appointment to someone who was now sitting ram-rod stiff with a stern, vindictive scowl on her face. And her body was now making violent jerking motions as she tried in vain to sit quietly in her chair. It was scary to watch this, and I knew by then what was happening. I wondered what was going to happen next.

This once-serene woman jerked violently a few times and then suddenly and abruptly leapt to her feet. To the stunned surprise and shock of the group, she began roaring disconnected phrases in a powerful and husky male-sounding voice. If you saw the movie *The Exorcist*, you have a pretty accurate idea of what was going on in that room, albeit on a lesser scale. The woman stomped into the center of our circle and began preaching to us loudly, using powerful hand, fist and arm gestures, all the while quoting unintelligible religious-sounding phrases. It sounded like she/he/it felt we were all messed up and needed a healing, and that she/he/it was just the one to perform that duty.

She wheeled abruptly, turning to the nearest person seated in the circle, a woman (there were about five men in the group), and proclaimed to this woman that she/he was going to do a healing on her and was she ready. I think the woman in our group was too shocked to do anything but agree. This moments before gentle, soft spoken woman visitor had now transformed into a raving, belligerent, inconsolate old man. She was making stiff, jerky body gestures like those of an agitated old man and she poked the air wildly when he/she wanted to make a point. Then Jan/he began speaking more clearly and we understood, in a fashion, what he/she was trying to impart. No one moved. Everyone was spellbound, riveted to their seats.

I wasn't sure about the others, but personally I was getting increasingly angry and offended by these actions. The entity, whoever or whatever it was, had no right in any way to do what it was doing. I wanted to do something—anything—to stop this. But it was Ellen's group. Then to my still further astonishment, Ellen next agreed to the demands of the entity that the whole group be healed, one by one.

The entity, or Jan, started on the other side of the circle about eight people away from me. Jan/the entity stood in front of each person reciting what seemed to me senseless incantations, then grasped them in wrestling positions and poked her fingers into their mouths and ears. She made each person stand, sit or lie in contorted positions, all the while making powerful hand and arm gestures. It was bizarre. "She" continued to rave those crazy, quasi-religious phrases. She was coming closer to me, person by person. I felt trapped and was growing increasingly nervous. Finally it was my turn. The entity demanded in a bellowing tone if I wanted to be healed. Quickly, I replied resolutely with a flat no. I then

The Light of the Creator Force

added in an angry tone, "You are not going to do anything to me! Don't even touch me!" I was the only one in the room who made any effort to refuse a "healing."

The possessed woman stood statue-like with an insanely wild expression of confusion on her face. My refusal had been completely unexpected. Several times, as she stood in front of me the woman's face began to slowly transform. There was a back-and-forth battle going on inside for possession of the body between the intruder and its owner.

I need to mention here that I am not exaggerating this incident even a bit. This activity was witnessed by the seventeen other people in the room.

The possessed woman stood speechless for a few moments. The entity had not at all anticipated my reaction. She or it, then bent over me, staring wildly into my eyes, I could clearly see two totally different personalities in the one body. Jan's eyes would go from gentle to angry and back again, darkness and light behind her eyes. The inner struggle for dominance between the body's owner and the intruder continued.

I took the opportunity to speak to the possessing entity directly while it was still off balance. I said, deliberately and calmly, "You have no right to be in this woman's body. Why don't you get out of her body and leave her alone?" Instantly the entity was back in control. It rationalized in disconnected phrases: "Yes—no—she—because—because I—I am—I will—I want—I want to—I must." It went on this way for a minute or more. Several times Jan's face took on a desperate, pleading expression as she momentarily regained some control. Next addressing Jan I said, "Do you want the entity to leave your body? Demand it!" Almost at the same time the entity, once again dominant, shouted in a belligerent tone, "You need to be healed! You must be healed now!"

Then, without my permission it/she seized my hands forcefully. Then my knees. Then the entity put one hand on my forehead, all the while reciting more nonsensical Biblical sounding phrases. She/it then pushed two fingers of her other hand in my mouth! That was it for me and I started to react. Before I could make a move, it must have anticipated my anger and it quickly went on to the person sitting to my right and began with that person another senseless tirade of words and hand movements.

I still could barely believe what was transpiring. No one argued with or resisted the entity, not even Ellen. She got a healing too. The possessed woman eventually went one by one all the way around the circle, finishing with the last person. "The entity" then walked to the center of the circle, continuing the defiant body postures and loudly preaching more religious sounding gibberish.

But Jan was slowly coming fully back into her body and she was looking ill, in fact, deathly ill. Her face had become a colorless white mask with a corpse-like pallor to it. Clearly, the situation was becoming extremely serious. *Finally*, Ellen realized the severity of the situation and decisively took command. She got to her feet and made Jan sit down. Ellen would not even let Jan speak. A blanket was spread on the floor and Jan was made to lie on her back. She looked absolutely horrible. There were a few people in the room who had some experience with possession and there was, coincidentally, an excellent chapter in *The Teachings of the Inner Christ* on possession and how to remedy it if it occurred.

It was over an hour before the people working on her could get Jan back to what one would consider normal. Jan finally got to her feet, herself again, but she was stunned and exhausted. She still was white as a sheet. Jan went home without keeping her chiropractic appointment. No—she didn't sue. It would have made an interesting court case wouldn't it.

This situation never would have or could have occurred if Jan had had even an elemental knowledge of discarnate beings and possession and of her absolute right to her own "space." She walked into that room wide open and vulnerable. But if one knows that possession can be real and understands it somewhat, no one ever needs to be affected by it.

Again, if we have a theme of goodness in our lives, believe in Spirit, know who we are and believe in and are happy with who we are, we will never have to worry about any kind of dark or negative force, however it might be perceived.

Unseen Beings, Unseen Worlds

*"The world is not only stranger than we suppose, it is stranger than we **can** suppose."*

— J.B.S. Haldane

Chapter 5

Another Strange Case of Possession

As a side note to Jan's ordeal there was, several weeks later, a similar, related occurrence which no doubt ties in directly with Jan's unfortunate encounter. There was at the time a successful young doctor who on several occasions came to our open, introductory classes. These classes were held every other week in addition to our regular classes. The extra classes were casual and were open to anyone who wanted to see what the teachings were about. These open sessions were simple and informal and usually were devoted to guided meditations, channeling practice and then a period of discussion on whatever subject was of interest.

During one of our regular classes a short time after the Jan melodrama I had again seen in the room what I thought to be a negative astral. It radiated a very unpleasant feeling. I mentioned the entity to the class and drew for them a diagram of what I saw. These astrals such as the one that approached the class appear to me to have a form, a shape, like a black and white bull's-eye, sort of like this:

I have seen many variations of this bull's-eye pattern and the larger, blacker ones without question seem to be the more powerful. The bull's-eye pattern may not at all be an astral's actual form but may be the way my subconscious sees the astral and interprets it to me. It's interesting that I rarely see any of these astrals in new cities like the cities in  the western states. However, I often see and detect them in old cities such as those in New England. The astral I saw that day in the room near the group, was three to four feet in diameter. The smallest ones that I have seen are about six inches in diameter. I've never seen one smaller than six inches. I assume that the amount of power they have corresponds to their size. There is also the possibility that they can, at will, alter their size.

After Jan's experience, the class and I were somewhat disturbed by my second sighting of the entity (others had also "felt" the entity) but we went on with the class as usual anyway.

Up until now I haven't mentioned third eye vision which would normally be assumed to be involved here. Here's why. I think that the third eye concept that has been popular for so long is far from being accurate or correct. I don't think any human *ever* had a third eye in the middle of his forehead and I do not think clairvoyant vision originates from the front or middle brain area. Rather, I believe, based on from my own personal experience, that psychic seeing actually originates from the invisible whole self. Or in other words, the etheric *whole* self functioning on the soul level. The soul, by definition, is the part of us that is our current personality and character and that lives on after our physical bodies die. The inner living self or life force sees all. The seeing comes from the entire part of us that is not physical. The etheric soul part of us sees all in every direction, dimension and time.

Along with the third eye concept came the interesting practice of trepanning. Trepanning was once quite popular, particularly in Peru. It is still to this day practiced in a few left-wing or right-wing cult religions all over the world. The South American Indians once did a lot of it. Trepanning is basically drilling or boring a hole through the forehead so there is less obstruction and this supposedly frees up the third eye so it can see better. Sometimes I wonder who starts ideas like this and finds individuals gullible enough or willing enough to submit to and continue the practice. Trepanning does indeed continue to this day. It probably does work very well in opening up a person's clairvoyant ability because a participant wouldn't want to have another hole drilled in his or her head. Fear is always a great motivator, among other things.

So the young doctor, who was about 30 at the time, sat in on our open *Teachings of the Inner Christ* classes. This was about the same time period as the Jan experience, give or take several weeks. He was sincerely interested in taking the full course at a later date. I'll call him Don. We didn't see Don again for several weeks for he was busy constructing a large and expensive two-story office building which was to be a center for medical practitioners. I was at that time a channel and was teaching people how to be channels for ascended masters or high-level spirits. My classes were always full. I was extremely busy at the time with a variety of unrelated matters and had no thoughts about Don. One day some weeks after I had last seen Don, a woman in my channeling class who knew Don well had some disturbing news. Shortly after the last open session Don had attended, he had begun acting completely out of character. He missed important meetings with architects, building contractors, bankers and fellow associates involved in the building project. He became introverted, insolent, sullen and argumentative. This was especially disturbing because he was normally a pleasant, cheerful, helpful and relaxed person.

Astral possession came immediately to my mind. I remembered the appearance of the astral in the room about the time Don had been there. The timing of the different events seemed to me far more than just a coincidence. Don's abrupt behavior was all too typical of low astral possession. His career and office building venture would shortly be on the rocks, I was told, along with an enormous loss of borrowed money. When last seen, he had driven off down the coast toward Big Sur and hadn't been in contact with his associates for ten days.

At that time, several evenings a month, I held public channeling sessions at my home. One evening I had just finished a long and exhausting channeling session to a full house. I remained where I sat doing deep breathing and recentering exercises. Twenty or thirty people were still mingling, socializing and getting their coats. I was facing the front door, I saw Don slip quietly in through the open door and come in my direction. Don didn't look good. In fact, he looked terrible. I don't think he had changed clothes in a week. He pulled a chair up in front of where I was sitting, and said quietly, matter-of-factly, "Tom, I need help." If I can do something of help for someone I am glad to do it, but I have a deep apprehension of giving someone wrong advice lest they end up in deeper trouble, injured or worse. I replied to Don's statement with, simply, "I know." Then added, "Do you want to hear what I have to say?" He nodded that he did. He had a tired, sober expression on his face.

Don had already heard about the Jan incident and was familiar with it, but I went back over it in detail for him so that he had a good clear mental picture of what had happened that night. I cautioned him that I could very well be wrong, but that it was my opinion that the same entity that had possessed Jan was now influencing him. Don had visited the group several times and somehow, I said, the astral had perhaps also attached itself to him. Don was ready for *any* kind of positive advice by that time and the idea of possession seemed entirely possible, even likely, to him. His life had become absolute hell, he told me, and it had all come on so suddenly. Don was that evening completely open to what I had to say—that he could well be under the possession of a discarnate entity.

Openness to change is a decidedly positive attitude for rectifying a particularly unpleasant situation a person may be enduring. I knew that what I had to recommend might not work but at least he believed in what I said and was willing to give my remedy a try. I told Don that first of all, if this was a case of possession, the entity had no right whatever to have control over him and it was up to him to demand with complete conviction that the astral leave his auric field so that he could get on with his personal affairs. I also suggested

Another Strange Case of Possession

that Don ask for help from high spiritual sources and that he see himself filled and surrounded with the brightest white light that he could visualize. It was important to see every cell of his body blazing with this white light. To reiterate, this white light visualization works, whether it is the effect of actual white (spiritual) light or it is the subconscious taking command and correcting a particular situation or both. Or it may be something else. At any rate it works.

The astral entity had a name. I had gotten it psychically from the entity at the time of the Jan incident and I related the name to Don. He seemed to feel that the two-syllable, Arabic-sounding name was correct. It's also interesting to note that I mentioned the astral name to a number of people without telling them it's origin, and the general reaction was that mentally repeating the name gave them the creeps.

I told Don to speak to the entity, in silence or out loud, telling it that it should move on to the next level where all along, it was supposed to be. I told Don to ask for high spiritual help and to remind the astral that it was "dead" and had lost its physical body. The being needed to be reminded that it was no longer a physical being. It was wrong for it to remain on the Earth plane and it had to go on. And, I said, if the astral itself would ask, a spiritual being would come and guide it to its new level, a good and beautiful place where it would feel love, safety and comfort. Don agreed to try my suggestion and left the room as quickly and as quietly and as unobtrusively as he had entered. I was still extremely busy and preoccupied at the time with a number of projects, so in the following weeks gave little thought to Don's problem. After our meeting I felt that I had done my best.

About a month after Don had met with me, someone who knew Don intimately and saw him often brought me some good news. I was told that Don was his old self again. He had salvaged his practice and the new building project and everything was proceeding along with exceptional smoothness. Don is today a very successful doctor.

Whether or not the advice I gave Don was the solution for his problem, I will never know for sure, as I never saw him again, but one day months after our conversation I got a note from Don that simply said "thanks." This light, knowledge, request and affirmation procedure works. Until something better comes along it seems to be the best method we have. Whenever possible, I also always recommend for the person hypnosis by a qualified professional who knows how to deal with possession if possession appears to be the problem.

In some countries, such as those in South America, possession is treated with an attitude of genuine seriousness, even by many medical doctors. It is not maligned and shoved under the rug as it typically is in this country. In a number of countries, particularly Brazil, hypnotic regression is commonly used as therapy in many cases of neurosis, multiple personality disorder and schizophrenia. In a hypnotic regression session purposefully dealing with entity possession the possessing entity(s) will usually surface, speak to the hypnotist, and be convinced or reminded by an *experienced* therapist that the possessing entity is dead, no longer has a body of its own and has no right to be occupying the patient's body. The entity must be convinced to leave and go on to where assistance and a better place awaits it. This can take many sessions. Some astrals are exceedingly reluctant to vacate a borrowed body because it is a safe haven and hiding place for them, a refuge.

There is also an associated situation where a discarnate human openly and freely chooses to remain on the Earth plane for a while and has no interest in or intention of occupying or bothering an incarnate person. The being may simply want to hang around for a while and be near its Earth family or a home or location he or she loved. It might be that these entities enjoyed their lives so much they just don't want to leave yet. When they are ready, they go on. I have talked to these spirits or ghosts or astrals, whatever one wants to call them. It isn't particularly difficult to talk to them, especially when you get past the initial fear of the experience. (I'll tell you how in chapter seven) I have discovered, to my surprise, that some of them on the Other Side don't know much more than I do about the afterlife. They are now in a place that is often difficult for them to describe adequately. They have a semi-physical body, they don't need money anymore; some actually, on occasion, eat solid food like fruit, but never, never meat; they can travel instantaneously wherever they want to go—they just think it and they are there. There is no sickness or disease. There can be strong disagreements between them but never fighting (that I know of). I'm not speaking here of the inhabitants of the gray zone. That is another matter altogether. I'm speaking here of astrals, or spirits, that are free to travel freely and are generally of a pleasant disposition. If they don't have a pleasant disposition, chances are they won't speak to one of us, the "living," anyway. I may be getting a little too deep here. Some of these "astrals" may have crossed over all the way to a higher level and may be able to go back and forth and visit or stay back here as long as they want to. Of that I'm just not sure. It's interesting that some say that where they are now is almost identical to the Earth, except that where they are is incredibly beautiful and has none of the negative aspects of the Earth we know, the Earth they once inhabited. They sometimes find themselves in a body that, although now perfect, is almost as physical as their Earth body.

I am aware that all this can sound crazy to some people, especially those conditioned by religion, and for years I carefully avoided discussions about these topics for fear of ridicule and reprisal. I've had several occasions of fundamentalists becoming raving, beligerant, lunatics after merely overhearing a discussion about the paranormal I was having with another person.

Speaking about fundamentalists, this is a quote from a September 10, 1993 speech the Dalai Lama gave in Phoenix, Arizona:

"Under certain circumstances . . . there is danger if you have a fundamentalist attitude. Because this religion involves emotion . . . there is a danger there if someone gets so much emotion it hardly leaves any room for reason."

I have had many past encounters with the basic resident "house ghost" and they hold little interest for me anymore. I learn little or nothing from them. But I have learned much from the ones who can travel or move about freely. I enjoy this aspect of astral contact very much and still make contact as often as the occasion presents itself.

I suppose I might seem to be confusing the varied and different levels of the lower astral realm, what are perhaps levels one, two and three out of the ten levels, I mentioned before. I think that because of my physical, Earthly consciousness I simply have no way to realistically correlate to an existence that has nothing to do with material anything but instead is a reality of weightless energy and fleeting dimensions, and, as I will mention several times in the book, I won't and don't believe anything, regardless of the source, unless I can prove or validate the information to myself in some way. It doesn't matter whether the information comes from a book, a channel, a teacher or whatever.

I should mention here that one should never, ever, try to psychically fight a negative, aggressive predatory astral. One can't win — I have tried it. I have known and have read of others who have tried it — usually with disastrous results. Several times I challenged an astral when I was a psychic novice and luckily I think I am still in one piece. The head to head encounter to force the astral away will drain a physical body's energy to the point where it seems that even the life force is ebbing away — and maybe it is. One can't fight them but one can coax, cajole, reason and encourage them in a friendly helpful manner that will always get results. And nobody gets hurt. Either the astral takes the suggestion or it doesn't. I get mild amusement at times when I read or hear of people who try to "pull" astrals out of people or exorcise or drive them out. Good luck. Usually this just pisses the astral off and then the exorcist *really* has a problem.

I have tried it three times, fighting psychicly with astrals. It's like a psychic chess game or a duel with psychic swords and psychic energy. If one plays this game and loses, the cost can be too high. Sanity is often the price of defeat. This scenario also applies to willful collusion with a predatory astral, such as in some Satanic rituals. "Devil" takes on a real meaning here. Predatory astrals hold all the cards because the conflict is all on their turf. They can see you better than you can see them, they can manipulate energy far better than you can and they can attack and defend themselves far better than you can. And they don't have the decided disadvantage of a slow, bulky physical body. Take my advice, don't ever try it. Don't be around anyone who tries it. This is the deadliest game of all. The shamanic brujos in Central and South America are particularly noted for these direct confrontation kinds of radical exorcism/healing practices. However, I am sure from research that in the majority of cases(but not all of them) there is a high degree of profitable charlatanism involved by these practitioners. The patient walks away "cured" when there was no hard-core possession problem to begin with.

Unseen Beings, Unseen Worlds

"Look forward without fear to that appointed hour — the last hour of the body, but not of the soul; that day which you may fear as being the end of all things, is the birthday of your eternity."

— Seneca (4 B.C. - A.D. 65)

Chapter 6

Uh Huh — A Ghost!

The following accounts are examples of meetings and encounters I've had with discarnate humans and others. Several years ago I went along with a friend, Audrey P., to look at a house she was interested in purchasing in Cottonwood, Arizona. Cottonwood is a few miles south of where I live in Sedona. Audrey wanted my opinion of the house from a second person's standpoint. She was also aware of the clairvoyant things I do and the abilities I seem to have and wanted to know how the house "felt" to me in an energy sense. The house was basically an old ranch house built back in the 1940s. It had no furniture in it and was rather cavernous, as empty houses usually are. Audrey and a real estate woman were in the kitchen. I was standing in the living room near the open kitchen door. I wasn't particularly interested in what they were discussing and was daydreaming, when something to my right caught my attention. It was a powerful presence of a living entity and it was moving toward me. Sometimes unseen beings radiate so much energy that I can't help but notice them, even if I am totally preoccupied with thought at the time. This one did precisely that. The entity had come through the far doorway and stopped about ten feet to the right of where I stood. I turned and stared intensely in the direction of the unknown entity. My clairvoyant vision focused—I could sense unusually clearly in this particular case. It was a man—dead, of course. Audrey saw that I was concentrating with undivided attention on something in the room and said to me, interrupting the real estate woman, "What are you looking at?" I had no intention of mentioning the ghost but Audrey had brought it up, so reluctantly I told her. Some people can get weird, I mean psychotically weird, when you talk about these things and I did not personally know the real estate woman. Turns out she was a devout Baptist. I replied to Audrey in a matter-of-fact tone. "There is a man standing over there. He just walked into the room."

Without a second's hesitation, Audrey came back with, "You mean a ghost!" I answered, "Uh huh, a ghost."

The real estate woman sort of froze. Her eyes got bigger and her jaw slacked perceptibly. She was obviously wondering what kind of nuts she was with way out there in the country. She didn't turn her head, but her eyes looked for a fast route back to her car. She questioned in a flat monotone, "A ghost"?

"Yes" I said. "He is about five feet ten inches tall and has a full head of bushy snow-white hair. He has an enormous pot belly, he wears a white tee shirt and has on blue jeans."

The real estate woman turned pale and, totally flabbergasted, uttered, "That sounds like George Mason!!" (The name is a pseudonym.) "He was the last owner of this house! George died about six months ago of lung complications. He was a heavy smoker—two or three packs a day."

I asked George telepathically why he was still here. He replied reluctantly, obviously not at all enthusiastic about speaking to a "live" person. He telepathically said that he was waiting for his wife and would go on after that. I told Audrey and the real estate woman that George had said that he was waiting for his wife. I added that that didn't make much sense to me.

Uh Huh — A Ghost!

The real estate woman's eyes got even bigger and her jaw fell a bit more. She offered nervously that George's wife was still alive and was in a local rest home, but she was terminally ill and was not expected to live much longer.

George just stood there watching us. He wasn't impressed with us. Dead people usually aren't, for some reason, and avoid us if they can—at least the ones who were normal when they were alive. They will talk, but often they have to be prompted to do so after they see that you are sincere and not terrified of them.

The real estate woman suddenly regained her composure and exclaimed with let's-change-the-subject gusto, "Shall we go out and look at the rest of the property?" At that, she bolted out a side door and headed with long strides toward an open grassy area near her car. I gestured goodbye to George and wished him well telepathically. He made no effort at a response. He just stood there watching as I left. Very often ghosts are annoyed at being discovered and would much rather be left alone. George was one of those.

There are a lot of things that give off an energy feeling that can be mistaken for a ghost, such as ley lines, and particularly divergent ley lines that cross in a room. Few houses are really "haunted." If a house actually does have a ghost, and if asked I can usually find that ghost in a few minutes or less. Several days ago I was investigating extraordinarily strange paranormal activity at a remote Northern Arizona ranch. Part of this paranormal activity involved the owner's large dog who would occasionally look up and growl menacingly at something unseen in the house. I have no idea what it was. Dogs and cats staring or growling at something unseen is often a sure sign of ghost activity—or something else. Several times I've watched dogs and cats sit up and follow intently with their eyes something invisible moving around in a house.

For example, I had an interesting dog/unseen entity event happen to me once in the mountains near Santa Cruz, California. I was visiting friends at their home in Boulder Creek ten miles west of Santa Cruz. They had an Australian sheep dog that more resembled a bear than a dog. (In fact I think the dog's name *was* Bear.) I had just come from a class at the Berkeley Psychic Institute, which I attended, in which we had been doing some astral-related psychic exercises. I walked into the living room of my friends' home and the dog's eyes riveted on me instantly. The dog was always curious and friendly anyway, but this time it struck me as being rather odd. The dog sprang to his feet, came over to me, jumped up, put his paws on my shoulders and extended his head toward something behind me. I am 6'3". As I said, it was a big dog. The dog became as excited as he would have if his master had just come home from work at the end of the day. He wagged his tail and panted happily. He wasn't looking at me or even interested in me. The dog was looking at something three feet over my right shoulder and slightly behind me. Whatever it was, it made the big dog very happy.

In a similar vein, years later I was visiting with people at their house near Sedona and it was mentioned that one of the couple's children, a girl, had seen a ghost in the basement which was open to the west with large windows. She was terrified and would not sleep in her room down there. The little girl was about five years old. Very young children often have clear psychic abilities and vision; because they have not forgotten yet. The little girl's concern was taken seriously and I was asked if I would take a "look" at her bedroom. As we walked down the stairs into the basement I immediately sensed a ghost nearby. I also felt an overpowering radiation of fear from the ghost. Somehow the ghost knew that I was going to find it. In the middle room, which was a storage room, I found the ghost. (It is, at times, extremely difficult for me to see ghosts or to talk to them. Perhaps it has to do with my energy level or theirs.) The ghost was a woman about five foot in height, quite thin and with grayish hair pulled to the back of her head in a sort of pony tail. She was dressed in modern pants and blouse and was, when she was alive, about sixty or sixty-five years old. She said to me telepathically, anxiously, that she didn't mean any harm and she certainly didn't want to scare anyone. She just wanted to stay in the house with the residents. She was afraid that we would ask her to go away. I asked her what her name was. She replied that her name was Nita.

I related this information to the woman standing next to me and she said that that could only be Anita (nicknamed Nita), an elderly

Native American woman who had lived across from them at their former address in another state. Nita had especially loved the family's children because they had often gone to see her. Nita had died several years before and evidently, instead of going on to higher realms on the other side, had tagged along with the family in order to be near them. The woman told me to tell Nita that she was welcome to stay and that the family would not be afraid of her anymore. After that they had no more ghost problems. The children accepted Nita as one of the family. The little girl later drew several, all in white, portraits of Nita. Nita patiently posed for the little girl who could plainly see her.

About ten years ago in Maine, I had an extraordinarily unusual unseen being experience at the beginning of the opening up of my psychic abilities. I have not had this exact type of experience again although there have been several since that were in ways similar. It was in late summer while visiting in Southern Maine where I grew up, I was sitting in my sister-in-law's living room one night with several friends and relatives. There were four of us and we were experimenting with psychic phenomena. One of the women, a businesswoman, possessed quite advanced natural clairvoyant abilities. We were dabbling that night with different psychic type energies and auric field manipulation when suddenly we realized we weren't alone. An additional and odd factor was that it was exactly midnight. It was rather chilly in the room; I believe there had been a cold rain earlier in the evening. We realized that we had been joined by "others" who were now in the room. They were invisible to the eye but radiated an incredibly cold energy which made it very easy to follow their movements around the room. We found five of them. None of us could see them but we could feel "them". We all could. And they definitely moved. We could easily locate them and follow them around the room because of the basketball sized area of coldness they radiated. What was coldness to our human senses may not necessarily have been negative in any way but it was certainly their "body" energy. By cold, I mean dry-ice cold. We could follow the entities movements by walking slowly around the room with our arms extended and our hands open. The entities drifted around the room slowly, methodically and intelligently. If we were sitting or standing still and one of them brushed past us it was quite an experience, believe me. I have recently, late 1993, found other people who have had identical experiences in different parts of the country.

The initial encounter with and discovery of these unusual visitors happened while I was sitting opposite the others and demonstrating how to expand and contract an auric field. The two women in the room were able to psychically see this shifting energy around my body. I was sitting on the sofa concentrating on expanding and contracting my auric field when I became, without warning, aware of an extremely cold radiation which seemed to originate from somewhere out in front of me. I opened my eyes and extended one hand straight out. I touched something that was incredibly cold. I felt with my hands its dimensions and it was nearly round, with a diameter of about one foot, about the same size as a basketball. The thing was suspended in the air and was very slowly moving. I knew "it" was alive. It was then about four feet away but suddenly it started moving directly toward me. I put out the other hand with my arms fully extended and my hands open wide in an instinctive defense posture. I was trying to hold it away from me. It flowed *through my hands* and in seconds touched my face and flowed around my head and onto my shoulders. I was sitting there trying to analyze this eerie and weird sensation when the lady who was a natural psychic spoke with a measure of alarm. "My God, Tom, your face just disappeared!" At that, with little hesitation, I quickly stood up and went to another part of the room. I felt spacey. We played a sort of tag with these balls of energy, or entities, for about a half hour. Then they vanished. They were gone as quickly as they had appeared. I've learned that if I don't fear things like this, they have always been for me fantastic and wonderful learning adventures. Had we lost control when the beings arrived and been running around in fear and panic, could we have been attacked? I would have to say that that could have been a distinct possibility. But it didn't happen.

Everyone has varying degrees of psychic abilities. The main and basic reason most people never utilize them is because they don't really believe in their own psychic abilities and fear giving those dormant potentialities a chance. Psychic ability usually has to be worked at. It has to be developed by trial and error. One has to trust in it and trust what the inner self sees especially in association with unseen worlds. Encountering unseen beings and energies such as I just mentioned is part and parcel of psychic ability. I have noticed that in books and writings that deal with the topic of other-worldly beings, they always stress protecting yourself before attempting contact or communication. That is certainly excellent advice although, speaking for myself, I have always been a bit reckless when it comes to my own experimentation with highly paranormal worlds and entities. Either I have been just plain lucky or I do indeed have someone unseen watching over me. Another possibility that has been suggested several times is that I had a great deal of experience in dealing with paranormal realms in another lifetime or other places and developed or was taught a talent in these areas that I am now remembering or re-activating. Maybe.

About 1980 I had an experience that could illustrate the possibility that someone is watching over me. I am sure everyone has had experiences similar to this at some point in his or her life. For twenty years or so I was a serious and dedicated distance runner. In fact I was quite fanatic about it. One day in 1980, while out for a five-mile run in Verdi, Nevada, where I lived on the Truckee River, I came close to a serious mishap on a bridge that crosses over the Truckee.

I had finished about two-thirds of my run when I looked down and noticed I had a loose shoelace on my right shoe. I normally never stopped during a run unless I absolutely had to. This time, almost automatically, I stopped running, went to one knee and began adjusting the shoelace. I remember thinking how uncharacteristically odd this was because I could have easily finished my run with the lace as it was. I heard a car coming. I looked up and saw a light blue car approaching rather fast with a young woman at the wheel. The car crossed the wide cement bridge and as it came to my side of the bridge, about seventy-five yards from where I was, the car wandered onto the sandy shoulder. The woman, suddenly seeing she was off the pavement, wildly overcorrected and the car spun around broadside across the two-lane highway. In a second the car flipped over, as it did it bounced straight up ten feet, sailed hundreds of feet upside down, went down a long, steep embankment, over some small trees and landed in a soft, watery marsh. On impact the driver was thrown out of the car into the marsh and was completely unhurt except for being soaking wet.

Several days later I carefully retraced and repaced my course near the bridge. I discovered, with wonderment, that if I had not stopped to fix the shoelace when I did, I would have been on the exact spot where the car had spun sideways and flipped over.

Similarly, when I was in my twenties I had two friends, Rick and Brian, who were like brothers to me. The three of us did almost everything together. One evening they stopped to pick me up to go into town and for some reason I did not want to go with them. We even got into an argument about it. I refused to go. They drove off without me and three hours later they were both dead in a car accident that was so terrible the only part of the car that was still in one piece was the engine.

Years later, a friend whom I normally would have been with at that particular time fell asleep at the wheel of his car and went off the road. The car cut a telephone pole in half and the upper half spun around on the wires and came down through the roof where I would have been sitting. He was unhurt.

It seems someone wants to keep me around for a while. One of the reasons, I hope, is to write books like this. There have been at least another half dozen similar but unrelated events akin to the aforementioned three.

Abraham Lincoln believed in spirit communication, and was guided and counseled by statesmen from the spirit world during his troubled times. That the Lincoln's held seances at the White House a great deal, was well known, the medium most often being the extraordinary Nettie Colburn. After he was installed in office, the newspapers linked him with Spiritualism, remarking that he had been seen going to certain meetings. And when a reporter from the *Cleveland Plain Dealer* asked him if this was slander, he replied: *"The only falsehood is that half has not been told of the wonderful things I have witnessed."* In the book *Willie Speaks Out – The Psychic World of Abraham Lincoln* we read that he received many evidential messages from his son Willie in the spirit world.

Chapter 7

How to Talk to Spirits

I do indeed think that some type of protection is in order and certainly wise when one attempts to link up with the unseen and go beyond into the unknown. Again, protection can be worked in a number of forms. Asking a high spiritual being to watch over one, placing white light in and around the body, and using solid, clear-cut affirmations of protection are fine.

I would include here a caution about affirmations. People tend to be a bit wishy-washy about their convictions in an affirmation—in other words, vague, ineffective and doubting. Just saying the words won't do the job. One needs to be definite, decisive and forceful when using affirmations.

I was once given an affirmation and visualization technique I would like to share here with everyone. This was given to me by a woman who is a psychic healer. She travels the world alone and has had amazing "protection" down through the years. I have, over time, tried hundreds of affirmations and this is the only one I use gularity. It seems to work well for me. Others may have a better one. It is as follows:

"I am filled and surrounded with the blazing white light of the beloved Creator. Nothing but good shall come to me. Nothing but good shall go from me. I give thanks. I give thanks. I give thanks. So be it"

Another method that works well for me is to fill my body with white light expanding to several feet out and then visualizing a layer of sparkling gold energy covering the white.

I also frequently use the Tibetan Ascended Master, Djwhal Khul's Ring Pass Not visualization of protection. I simply see a bright ring of white light around myself, three or four feet out, and affirm that any entity who would do me harm in any way cannot pass into the center of this ring.

These do seem to work very well for me. They are just several suggestions. There are many, many good ones in many, many books.

So now we are ready to begin to talk to spirits. To go into this with a lot of curiosity and a complete lack of fear and paranoia will help the process immeasurably. As we all know, fear on its own will generate many events and situations. We can create monsters that are entirely real to the mind but that in actuality do not exist at all. Higher beings on the other side are, for the most part more than willing to converse with us, especially once we get good at it. In a way it's like learning a foreign language. Eyes can be open or closed when doing this procedure. Sometimes it takes a great deal of concentration and in those instances I always keep my eyes closed. Sometimes the connection is so easy I can sit with my eyes open and talk freely and effortlessly with the unseen entity. That is when the experience is especially fun and educational.

When I communicate with unseen beings I usually wait until one happens by, like a pedestrian walking along, or until one is drawn by the "signal" I put out, a signal that I want to speak with an advanced being from Over There. For some reason I have never stayed very long with the same personality or entity. I prefer variety. Although, if I try hard enough, I can usually "call" a being whom I have talked to before. This is usually at the insistence of someone here, human on the Earth plane, who wants to talk to that particular being Over There. (Don't get me wrong, I don't do this all day every day. Two or three times a month is typical.) Sometimes I get a name from a being I am talking to and sometimes not. I have discovered that some of them are not in the least interested in names (labels). I think most, if not all, of them do have a name of sorts. But I get the impression that most of them Over There in the invisible realms recognize each other by individual vibration. When they want to talk to someone else Over There somewhere, what they do is feel and think and visualize that other being's vibration. The called being feels and sees that call and comes to the summons if it can.

I'm not sure how much actual distance there is between those of the unseen worlds and us, at least distance in the way we might think of it, like forty million miles or something. The distance, in reality, may be vast or it may not exist at all. It is better not to think in terms of distance, putting it out of mind. If we think in terms of distance it will hinder us. We first focus in our minds with certainty that we can have and will have a beneficial link with the Other Side. We know that we can easily bridge the gap that separates the worlds. If you don't believe you really can do all this, you never will. But when you know and believe with confidence and conviction that it really is as simple and as easy as picking up a phone and talking to someone, then it will work. Simple. Simplicity is always the key. Never assume anything when dealing with the other side, no preconceived notions or ideas, just let it happen. It will *always* be different from what one expects. We humans tend to intellectualize things to death. We should remember simplicity, and not strain. This process should be as easy as we can make it.

When I begin the initial contact with an unseen being I always see developing in my mind (it might turn out to be different for others) a rather foggy bluish-colored void. In a few minutes a being will usually approach and enter into this void. It's very important that my mind be relaxed, rather indifferent and in neutral. I don't strain. I can't have ten competing thoughts jamming and confusing the process, such as what I am going to have for supper, the repair bill or some other distraction. I "feel" the being coming. They, Over There, radiate a vast variety of energies. This is easy now that I have become sensitive to it. Some of these beings, I have found, are more powerful, more wise and more knowledgeable than anything I can put into words. Some of them are just sheer, awesome power.

I see them in my mind usually in one of three ways. One, a luminescent, human-like form; two, a ball of light; or three, a clearly defined and detailed entirely physical looking human form. They may take the human form to make it easier to relate to them, or it may be that they were recently human somewhere and still retain that form. The ones that are orbs of light are *always* the great and powerful ones. The lightbeings (orbs) are the powerful ones and the lights can be any color or combination of colors. The colors are always incredibly beautiful and have a silvery radiance to them.

Now, once I feel or see a being nearby who is willing to converse, it is important that I avoid thoughts of being lowly, insignificant or unworthy. If I see myself as I did in the early going as a mere meek, insignificant human, hoping, on my knees, to talk to some lofty and regal superior being, chances are they won't even bother to make the effort to connect—at least not for long, anyway. We shouldn't worship them, prostrate ourselves before them or be supplicating to them, but polite and respectful—yes. If we will honestly make a determined effort to mentally talk with one of these beings as an equal, as a serious student, we will get rewarding and satisfying results. Sometimes they have to be extremely patient while we grope with the process but if they see that we are really in earnest and sincere they will in most cases try hard to accommodate us. If we *believe* that it is possible to speak to them, *it will be.*

I have found, and I have done this quite often, that what greatly aids this process is having a close friend present who will ask specific questions through me and then wait for the answer from the spirit being. The back-and-forth process will be clearer and easier. I have never had an experience with this with what might be termed a negative entity. But if the contact feels bad in any way, break off contact at once, drop it for that day and then try it again at a later date. Having other live people in the room somehow makes the signal clearer and stronger.

This is in a way like channeling, but the big difference is that one doesn't go into any kind of trance or altered state. Another definite advantage of this direct contact method over channeling is that I can mull over and think about the being's answer before I relay it to the listener. Sometimes after hearing the answer I may not *want* to relay it to the questioner at all. I have been in this situation a number of times and often the spirit being will leave it entirely up to me. I might choose to rephrase the answer so it will be more palatable to the one who asked. Spirit beings I have discovered can be very, very blunt. I mean no sugar coating, point blank, black and white, blunt.

Something that I do once in a while, although I don't print up flyers for this, is contact a "dead" relative to get vital information for a friend, or relative still here on the Earth plane. All I usually need is the full name of the dead person. It's really an incredible affirmation and reward when I get vital personal information that only the dead person could have known. I have now done this on many occasions.

The beings Over There, almost all of them, rarely communicate with each other in words. Over There they have a universal language that is instantly conveyed in feelings and pictures. They will rarely speak to us or to their own friends and associates in words. We have to get used to this. Also keep in mind that beings Over There don't sit around all day and night waiting for us to try to engage them in conversation. It's really quite low on their priority list, I think. Many of them, if not most, have a lot of things to do and may be taking time out of what may be an important and busy schedule to patiently try to talk with us. This is something that always bothers me about channeling. It must be, at times, an enormous imposition on a higher being when a human channel that particular being is committed to just sits down and starts channeling with no prior request for time of the higher being or any mental notification by the channeler. We need to treat them with the same courtesy, respect and diplomacy we would give to a respected, cherished and honored friend. Some beings are always absolutely delighted and charmed to get a chance to interact with us, but then there will be a few who will be short and impatient with us. Just like Earth people, a personality is a personality, here or Over There in the invisible worlds. But to talk to and be in the direct light and presence of a Universal Entity who may be millions or billions of years ahead of you in evolution is a feeling of wonderment and awe that has to be experienced to be fully appreciated.

We all know the saying "one picture is worth a thousand words." It's true and that's basically how they communicate with each other in the invisible realms. We in turn have to translate those pictures and the feelings which go with them which they transmit to us. It's fun, especially once you get a rapid-fire, back-and-forth transaction going with a particular entity. (And the entity might never have been a human!) It takes a bit of trial and error for a while. The effort however, is always worth it. It is a real pleasure, when at times you get a being who is willing or able to talk to you freely in good clear English (or whatever your native language is). Maybe only one out of four entities will or can do this.

We tend to think of them as perfect and flawless. Some of them are close to that but from my experience I can tell you that most of them have a terrific sense of humor and many of them have a temper of sorts. They never fly off the handle and react to things the way we often do but they can get icy blunt and stern at times. I have on several occasions had them lose patience with me, cut the session off and leave at that point. Just like us, their patience does have its limits. I tell some dyed-in-the-wool spiritual people stuff like this and they are often aghast and insulted that an ascended master would have a spicy sense of humor or, God forbid, a *temper*! Believe it. Those of the higher realms are not that much different from us except that they have made all the mistakes we are making now. They have gone beyond these mistakes and they are not about to get too close to the earth cycle and get caught up in it again. I have seen that they do often differ and disagree with each other. It takes the form of a friendly and mature disagreement. At the higher levels they never have shoving and shouting arguments. I've listened during a heated back-and-forth conversation, among two or more of these high entities debating a question in point. Usually, after a few minutes of rather intense banter, higher beings will settle on a consensus or just drop the whole matter altogether with no hard feelings. They know when to quit. These beings, once one gets used to their demeanor and appearance, are absolutely marvelous to be around, and the contact is *always* a fabulous learning experience. Once, in a question-and-answer session I had with four or five people in Colorado, a man, through me, asked an impossible question of a spirit. I think it was something about a personal relationship. There was a long pause and then the entity replied to me with a hearty chuckle, "He has got to be joking!"

By now I'm sure some readers are wondering how I have come to have this incredible ability but I don't know absolutely everything about everything. Anyone who gets into this will discover that there are some things that they of higher levels flat will not let us see or give us specific, exact information about. I ask hard, tough questions. They will instead, often give a generality and then clam up entirely when pressed point blank on a specific question. I have at times had them say, "We (or I) will not answer that" or they simply don't answer at all. Silence. This really irritates some people who want to know everything past, present and future, right now. We are here to discover and to learn. If invisible entities told us everything we wanted to know, they would probably be defeating the very purpose of why we, as humans, are alive here on the Earth. I firmly believe now that all of them who have earned great knowledge and wisdom are bound by some sort of law or regulation that they cannot (at this time) under any circumstance divulge certain information to us. We must find out these answers on our own. "Seek and ye shall find." They, Over There, cannot violate, under severe penalty, these nondisclosure-to-Earth-humans rules. That's how it works. This is not a free ride and we have to work hard to get out of here and to earn the right or privilege to be where the great spiritual ex-humans go. They earned the privilege and now, in turn, so do we. Yogananda, Yukteswar, Djwhal Khul, Babaji, Dadaji, Lahiri Mahasaya and Kuthumi are some of those who were human like we are and gained the knowledge and wisdom and love to leave here and to go to a higher, grander place.

There is I think, but I am not positive, some kind of a simple "secret." It's the ticket out of here. I'm not precisely sure what "it" is but I have been ever so close to discovering it on several occasions. All of the Great Masters who are now no longer physically among us had discovered or were told that secret. I think more of us long ago would have discovered the Secret except that we come from either such a deep profit framework or a deep intellectual motivational framework that we simply cannot see the Secret. The Great Secret. Simple. Look closely at the photographs of the few great masters who have allowed their pictures to be taken. Look at their facial expressions. I think it is pretty evident that they know what the secret is and are leaving the rest for us students to discover for ourselves. Yes, indeed, love is part of the secret, but love is only a vital component of it. There's more.

When I, hopefully, earn or gain the right to learn "it", I am out of here. I'm just being practical. (I am not one who believes all is perfect no matter what form it takes. That may work for some but not for myself. I need to categorize.) I know this ain't where it's at. I've seen what it's like Over There and personally that's where I want to be and to stay.

So, talking with beings on the other side is not particularly difficult but one has to work at it. Practice it. Good luck.

Camille Flammarion, the distinguished French astronomer, was a medium himself. He was President of The Society for Psychical Research, and in three published volumes he cites many authenticated messages received and visions seen, sometimes when thousands of miles separated the people concerned. He declared, *"Telepathy exists just as much between the dead and living as between the living."*

Chapter 8

How to Learn Remote Viewing

I have in the past refrained from teaching remote viewing, even though I've often been asked to, because I know what a few people would do with it. They would use it for the advancement of themselves at the expense of another. In other words they would spy on someone. I am going to explain how to do remote viewing here and I am going to ask that, once learned, this ability never be used to hurt or take advantage of another person or sensitive creature in any way, shape, form or manner. I won't go into it in depth in this book, giving examples, but if we use a God-given gift or privilege like remote viewing for greed, revenge or any form of destructive negativity we will in time pay a dear and great price for it. It's the Universal Law. The way it is.

So that it is clear that I am not blowing smoke about remote viewing and how it works (and that I know how it works), I'll give readers the opportunity to validate the existence of it for themselves. It's been satisfactorily proven by Russian and American researchers that remote viewing is not a psychic ability. It is a psychometric ability that can be taught to anyone, at least anyone who has a serious desire to learn the technique and commit to it a measure of dedicated effort. I learned remote viewing more or less by accident. In the remote viewing business I am known as a "natural". These following examples indicate my use and knowledge of remote viewing.

In the winter of 1991 I had gone to meet Tom O'Donnell, a psychologist friend, who was staying at a local motel. We were going to go to lunch. But I had to wait for Tom as he was still typing up a patient's report on his lap-top computer. While waiting, I sat on a bed and started browsing through a travel magazine. My mind quickly began to wander, as it often does, and I found myself daydreaming about nothing in particular. Tom owned a home near Durango, Colorado. The house sat on a high mesa and had a splendid, sunny, dining room that looked out onto the Animas River Valley. All of a sudden, to my surprise, I found my daydream centered on that dining room, and the vision of the dining room was so clear and vivid it seemed as though I were actually there. I found that I was looking down at Tom's large oak dinner table. The sun was shining on it brightly. Along with that I had strong visual impressions of the entire contents of the room and the rooms adjoining it. The early afternoon sun flooding through the windows gave the scene a rather smoky, eerie and alive feeling.

During this lucid vision of the dining room something drew my attention to what was lying on the far right corner of the dining room table. "Looking" closer I saw that it was my first two books, *The Mysteries of Sedona* and *The Alien Tide*. Looking still closer I saw that one book was on top of the other and they were both face down. The visual impression of all this was so clear and brilliant it disturbed me. I had never before experienced anything like this. This was just not normal. There was something entirely different about this daydream. I thought about the vision for a minute and then interrupted Tom as he worked at his computer. I said, with a great degree of hesitation and reservation, "Tom. At home, did you leave two of my books on the right corner of your dining room table, face down?"

He stopped typing, thought about it, then replied, "Why yes, I believe I did. I don't know if they were face down but I think I did leave them on the table." Then he asked why I had asked.

I answered that it was odd but I thought I could actually see the books there. He was intrigued by what I said and asked if there was anything else I could see. (As a psychologist he knew about remote viewing; at the time I had never even heard of the term.) While "standing" there in the far-away dining room and "looking" (I could do this in the motel room with my physical eyes either open or closed), I swung my rather foggy, dreamlike gaze and discovered I could not only see everything in the far-away room but could "float" around in any direction or any angle I desired to get a better or closer look at anything in the house. It was a wonderful and new experience but quite frightening at the same time. I, or at least part of me, was actually and literally in that dining room 350 miles away in Colorado. Yet I was, at the same time, sitting in the motel room in Cottonwood, Arizona. The part of me that was there in Durango gazing about in that far-away room could see with complete but dreamlike full-color clarity every single item within range of what would be normal sight.

Tom had at the time recently completed a glass-enclosed greenhouse, part of which now abutted the dining room. You had to look through the dining room and greenhouse windows to see the mountain and valley panorama outside. As a final touch he had stocked the greenhouse with tropical plants, birds and fish. I floated, with no effort except the desire to do so, through the dining room, through the living room and with no resistance through a closed glass door into the new greenhouse. I had never seen the greenhouse and had no prior exact knowledge of its contents. While floating (it felt absolutely comfortable and weightless) through the greenhouse I described the species and colors of every single one of the half dozen or so birds that were flying free in the temperature controlled greenhouse. I described the number and sizes of the Oriental goldfish in a small corner pool. Many of the tropical plants were in bloom and although I had no idea what the plants were, with 100% accuracy I described the colors, shapes and sizes of the flowers. If I wanted a closer look I found that effortlessly I could glide to within inches of whatever I wanted to look at.

The birds in the greenhouse got very spooked and nervous when I did this to them. I tried this experiment several times months later with Tom's small dog, Binky. Binky would stare straight back at me, acting like the whole thing was perfectly normal. Tom and I were *both* amazed at what happened that day at the motel. We agreed to do some in-depth experimenting with this odd discovery at a later date.

In the ensuing weeks I found that I could "go" to Tom's house with ease at any time of the day or night. On "arrival" I always found myself outside the house, high over a point above his driveway and looking down at his two-story home. I would then drift around until I located Tom. With a bit of concentrated effort I could almost always get his attention. This was getting to be great fun for both of us—especially me. When I "dropped in," usually in midafternoon, Tom was usually either out working in his garden, doing something in the kitchen or working at his computer. Unless he was completely preoccupied I could often telepathically let him know I was going to call him on the phone soon. (Sometimes he was where he couldn't hear the phone ring.) I would do this by bugging him to get his attention. I would telepathically shout something like, "Hey Tom, it's Tom. I'm going to call you at 3:30," or something like that. After a while he could recognize when I was around. Often he would stop what he was doing and go to the phone just as it rang.

I've tried this with other people with mixed results, but Tom and I got very good at it. I was always careful not to drop in at odd or unscheduled times so as not to intrude on Tom's privacy, which I did do on several early occasions when I was trying out this newfound phenomenon. What I was doing with these experiments was additionally interesting for me because I think it is almost exactly what spirits deal with when they want to get our attention or talk to us. During these visits I was a "spirit" myself.

Tom and I decided to do a sort-of-scientific, sort-of-clinical test of my developing remote-viewing abilities. We selected a day a week in advance. He was to collect a variety of different items and objects selected by him and which were completely unknown to me. He was to arrange this stuff in his living room. At the appointed time I was to travel there and try to remote view the objects he had readied for me. The day came. It was a Thursday. The agreed-upon time was 4:30 in the afternoon. Always one to do things a little differently, I decided I would "go" up to Durango a half hour early and eavesdrop. I thought I might get a preview of the odds and ends he had arranged for me in the living room. Tom is a bit of a nonconformist himself so I figured I'd stay a step ahead of him.

I arrived as usual over the spot above the driveway, drifted downward and glided effortlessly through the wall of Tom's second story office. (If you think this sounds crazy, wait until you try it!) I went through his office and glided down and around the spiral staircase. As I got near the kitchen, which is on the ground level, suddenly and instantly I was seized by a feeling of absolute, utter panic. Some sort of unnameable psychic alarm was going off inside me. I had a feeling of terror. I felt as if I were going to be ambushed in some way. I stopped at once and looked around. I took my time, but everything seemed all right. I quickly brushed the feeling off. Simple paranoia. There was no reason for so much alarm. I continued on. Tom was in the kitchen dressed in a red plaid shirt, blue jeans and cowboy boots. He didn't know I was there. He was cooking something that smelled spicy and sweet. That has been the only time so far that I have psychically smelled anything. The feeling of alarm, although lessened, was still with me. It worried me and annoyed me. The feeling would not go away.

Could it be, I thought, that some unseen, unknown agency, perhaps even alien, that I could not see or sense was preparing to attack me here and now? After all, I was a complete and total rank novice at this. The nagging feeling of an ambush again was bothering me greatly. I picked up the phone and called Tom. I told him that I had already been there, I told him what he was wearing and asked him what it was that he was cooking. With some amusement and amazement he replied that it was barbecue sauce and he confirmed that he was wearing exactly what I had just described. Before I got to the ambush thing he mentioned that his dog Binky had run off earlier in the day and he was concerned about the dog's whereabouts. I paused for a second and then told him the dog was at the front door. I could see the dog through the walls. He put the phone down. I heard the front door open, then a laugh and a bark. Binky loved to take off. I could always locate Binky in a second. He didn't stand a chance when I was around.

Tom was supposed to be alone in the house at 4:30 on that Thursday afternoon. I said, "Tom, is someone in the living room . . . . sitting on the couch?" Sheepishly, he admitted that there was. He had asked, unbeknownst to me, a neighbor to come over and be a witness to the experiment. This was perfectly okay with me, and that evidently had been the reason for the ambush sensation. For some reason I could not see the neighbor at all but I could by then sense him. A little later, even with strained effort, I got the neighbor's physical appearance and clothing entirely wrong. I wasn't even close. *I could not see the man.* (Since then there has been some interesting conjecture on this occurrence.) It was then that I discovered that there were and are some things I can not see no matter how hard I try.

We then began the prearranged test. Tom had placed the eight or ten small objects on his living room coffee table. I could quite plainly see a tall green plant on the table and I said (we were still on the phone)that I could not see the other objects. The plant was too big. First hit! The last time I had been to his house he had not had a plant on or near the coffee table. Tom took the plant, a cactus, off the coffee table and placed it on the floor.

I soon discovered another peculiarity. I could only see objects that were in direct sunlight! (This is not always the case.) The objects he held up out of the direct sunlight were in shadows so dark to my vision that I could not make them out at all. Ultimately, I got about 50% of the objects correct. My best hit was when he held up a large, framed photo. This was a tough one but with concentrated effort I said that it was a face and it took up a large area of the picture. I said it was in a shiny copper frame and there was a tree in the photo to the right of the face. Tom returned with, "Well, you are basically right about the face and frame but there is no tree in the photo." Then a few moments later he realized there was an added factor. He said that a reflection of his ten-foot tall ficus tree was on the glass to the right of the face and that was the tree that I had seen. I was looking over his right shoulder as he moved the framed photo around in the sunlight so I could see it better. I kept saying things like, "a little to the right, to the left, up, down, now tip it forward" and so forth. I could see all of this clearly while he held the phone to his ear.

I could go on with many verified examples like this but I think you get the idea. Here, then, is how to learn to do remote viewing. It is very simple. It just takes the effort. If nothing verifiable happens at first, don't worry about it. Keep trying. In the beginning do not try this or talk about this with anyone who is going to ridicule you or make fun of you over it. That will kill it dead if you are a beginner because it will anchor in you a belief that remote viewing is not real and you can't do it. Self-confidence is shaky enough in matters like this. That is, without doubt, the biggest obstacle I had to overcome in remote viewing and especially in the early stages of psychic experimentation and communication with the other side. I had to *believe* that I could do it. A willingness to accept mistakes and failures and to keep trying are definite attributes. A thick skin sometimes helps, too. There is only one other non-military source that I know of that teaches remote viewing and the lengthy course that they offer is expensive.

Let's start gradually with a beginning exercise. If you know someone who lives a hundred miles or so away from you who is a person you respect and trust like mom or dad or a brother, sister, or close friend and who lives in an area or a house you love to go to, it will make it much easier for you. Deep familiarity with a place facilitates the process. Preferably, you should choose a place in a lovely and quiet country setting. It certainly could be a city setting too, if it's quiet. But a big city makes it more difficult because of all the distractions of traffic noises, horns blaring, sirens, aircraft, tires screeching, gunfire and so on. I need to emphasize that distance is not at all a limiting factor. If you live in California, for example, and your trusted friend lives in Georgia, that's fine, but a distance of 100 to 300 miles away seems to be a good practice distance at first. But don't be overly concerned about distance; don't let it restrict you. I have done remote viewing at a distance of over 6000 miles with verifiable accuracy.

Practice on your own, confidentially and by yourself at first. Choose a quiet, relaxed, unpressured time and in your mind, as in a daydream, go to the home of that trusted person, whom you have told what you are doing. It can be any location you choose but you must be *intimately familiar* with that location. At first it must be a place you have previously been to a number of times. Position yourself mentally on the front lawn where this person lives or on the porch, in a room, under a big shady tree or wherever it is comfortable and secure for you. Again, it has to be a spot you love and that you know intimately. Imagine yourself being there, for real, on that beautiful and enjoyable spot.

Now, while you are there at your chosen spot, "look" all around you just as if you are really there and you have eyes to see everything. What is the day like? Is it warm, cool, raining or foggy, windy or hot and humid, snowing or cloudy or sunny? Take careful note of all that you "see." Details. Is the grass a nice rich green. Is the sky blue or white overcast? Is there a gentle breeze stirring that makes leaves rustle and limbs sway back and forth? Is it beginning to rain? Snow? Whose car or cars are parked in the driveway? What colors are the cars? Are there kids playing in the pool, on the grass, or having a snowball fight? Are there flowers blooming in the garden? With your "vision" go and inspect things more closely. Move right up to them to get a better look. A clearer look. How many roses are blooming in the rose patch? Count them. Are they white, yellow, red or pink? Go up close and look. Forget that you are two hundred miles away and "be" there. Daydream yourself there vividly. Practice these examples. You may want to go to several different locations in one session—maybe your favorite place in the Great Smokies or the Rockies, perhaps a secluded cove on a lake—it can be anywhere that you have a fondness in your heart. Do these practice runs for a few weeks or until you feel you are ready to go on to the next step.

The next step would be to include the person whose house you have been "visiting." This person has to be willing to participate in your learning experience. Do all of this with an almost childlike attitude of fun and adventure with no pressure. While the person is on the phone (be sure not to call when he or she is getting ready to go to work or to bed, or is busy making dinner) ask him, after you have "looked," if the day is, for example, sunny but very windy. Does it look like it rained hard earlier because there seem to be several large puddles of water in the yard? Is there a pile of loam or fertilizer on the front lawn because you see something dark brown and mound-shaped? That looks like a big stack of new lumber near the shed; is someone building something near the garden? Is that a new yellow tablecloth on the dining room table? You will probably find at first that you get almost everything wrong except for one or two direct or indirect hits. Those one or two hits will make you a firm believer and you will want more, much more.

Unseen Beings, Unseen Worlds

"There is no security on this Earth; there is only opportunity.

— General Douglas MacArthur

Chapter 9

Meditation, Remote Viewing, Spontaneous Viewing and "Barriers"

When I was initially experimenting with remote viewing, one day a friend, while we were on the phone, asked if I could see anything unusual near the front of the house. I was highly intrigued by the challenge and it was a fun and harmless test. I "looked" and "floated" around outside and replied that I thought I could see a large black and red mechanical object on the lawn. I hesitated with caution and ventured that I thought that it looked like a larger than usual garden rototiller. The exciting and gratifying answer was that it was indeed a large red and black garden rototiller. Direct hit! So that's it. That is how easy it is. You can use this ability to explore the world—free. I have. You can go to other planets, stars, galaxies and dimensions. You can visit alien civilizations or take a careful look at UFOs.

You can do just about anything as long as it is not harmful to anyone or anything, but be intelligent about it; this ability is not a toy. You will find that other-worldly entities will often detect you as soon as you arrive. Either you will be allowed and welcomed to stay or you will be warned away. The warnings are clear-cut and decisive. You will get the message loud and clear so heed those warnings. Don't hang around to see if they are bluffing, because they are not.

You will also discover that you will encounter areas that are off limits to psychic travelers and have barriers. These barriers are like glass shields or glass walls and *usually* cannot be penetrated. I won't go into these barriers in this book but I will say that they have been the subject of intensely serious research and probing by Russian and American scientists and certain American military intelligence units. I know the latter to be a fact because I heard it from a U.S. Army General during a lecture. The only reason he commented on it was that someone pressed him hard on the question. He was very reluctant to talk on that particular subject.

There aren't many drawbacks to remote viewing, but there are a few. Spontaneous viewing is one of them. You will be going about mundane daily activities and you will sometimes without warning or trying see something in your mind that is transpiring somewhere else. In a romantic relationship I had several years ago my girlfriend was seeing someone else at the same time and didn't tell me. It had been going on for months. In my mind I watched her having hot, x-rated sex with a man—and it wasn't me. Not a great way to find out, but as it turned out the mental pictures were 100% accurate. A great plot for a soap opera.

Remember, too, that in remote viewing you will not see things as clearly as you do with your physical vision. You will have to learn to see in a different way because in remote viewing, places and things are ethereal, rather hazy and dreamlike, although at times the scene or location can be razor-sharp vivid. A lot of what you see and experience you will have no way to validate but it will always be a great, exciting, experimental adventure. Good luck.

I think that in many ways remote viewing is similar to out-of-body experiences or out-of-body travel. I am not, for some reason, much interested in OBEs but am very well-informed on the subject. I

Meditation, Remote Viewing, Spontaneous Viewing and "Barriers"

would rather go "traveling" by keeping my mind, body and self in one place and look around by extension. In remote viewing you have far more control. There is a distinct and definite similarity and yet a distinct and definite difference between remote viewing and an out-of-body experience. If you have a curiosity about out-of-body experiences or a need to know, read Robert Monroe's books *Journeys Out of Body* and *Far Journeys*. Read *Journeys Out of Body* first as the books are one and two in a series.

Some sort of a background in meditation is an enormous advantage in enabling us to view or visit normally unseen worlds. It brings us closer to God, too. Meditation is important because it trains one to quiet the mind. A quiet, still mind is essential for higher spiritual or psychic learning. We have to control the runaway, spontaneous babble which often, perhaps usually, rules the mind. It is painfully difficult for most of us to sit absolutely still for ten minutes without our minds taking off in a stream of thoughts that go in twenty different directions. Controlling, or getting control of, the mind, is difficult for many of us, especially these days with all the worries and situations that we have to deal with. Perhaps some can keep in check the runaway thoughts of the mind without a background in meditation. That's good. It means they have very good patterns of discipline and are well on their way to being in a position to see the unseen and watch the watchers who constantly watch us. This, I think, goes hand in hand with meditation and a calm and peaceful mind. It's a doubly interesting experience for the reason that once unseen entities know that we can indeed see them during meditation and have gone to the effort to learn to see them, there is a tremendous amount of respect for us on their part. They aren't used to humans looking back at them.

Although they somehow know that we are first-grade beginners no matter how good we get at it, they will very often coax and encourage us along patiently so that we can expand our experience into their worlds. Most of them are happy to, more than willing to share their existence with us. They can do the magnificent things they do and why shouldn't we be able to do the same? When we finally, as a race, break free of the self-imposed chains that hold us suspended in time place we will, as a unit, join with them and they are glad for this also. I am sure. I am sure also that there have been nations or civilizations on Earth that have done just that in the distant past, civilizations and groups that have reached a state of perfection of spiritual and psychic consciousness, left their Earth bodies en masse and migrated to a better place somewhere Out There. These may include the residents of Anqkor Wat in Cambodia, Chaco Canyon (Anasazi) in New Mexico, Machu Picchu in Peru, and Tiahuanaco in Bolivia to mention just a few. It may well be that some of those same former Earth inhabitants are coming back to help us now. Hopefully, when they see that many of us are beginning to journey beyond the boundaries of the mundane, human, material world, they of the higher realms will stretch to give us all the assistance they can. But we have to move toward them; they *will not* do it for us. One step toward them, two steps towards us. I believe the Hundredth Monkey Principle will apply soon. It may be that one of us or someone else in some part of the world will be the hundredth monkey who sparks the spontaneous explosion that will free humanity from the bonds and chains of materialism and allow us to join the greater, liberated worlds of the unseen—in the unseen. This is all a part of meditation and meditation is part of the foundation that inspiration and innovation and creation spring from.

In meditation there are many methods and styles. For our purpose here I am not stressing reaching the Hindu samadhi euphoric levels of meditation. I don't think I have ever reached that state and it is, in my opinion, not essential for accessing the unseen worlds. Some spiritual or meditation books claim that samadhi is a necessary factor in reaching the higher worlds but I personally would find points of disagreement with that. My own meditation method utilizes the visualization of vibrant color. I don't meditate as often as I used to but in the beginning I had a meditation regimen which entailed sitting in a comfortable position for an hour or more every morning and visualizing filling my body, every cell, with vibrant, blazing, divine color. I did this for years. I use the colors red, blue, green, bluegreen, yellow, orange, violet, silver, white, pink and finally gold. It usually takes an hour to go from color to color. After

Meditation, Remote Viewing, Spontaneous Viewing and "Barriers"

a few months of this something in me began opening up and coming alive. That's the best way I (and others) can describe the experience. Sitting for a few minutes or an hour or more in the blackness of the mind either puts one to sleep or bores one so badly that one quickly loses interest in meditation. The mind needs something to work on, to concentrate on as we are meditating. For me it was working with colors. There are scores of excellent books on the market about meditation. In beginning meditation, we can choose a method that will work the best for us individually, a method that we are comfortable with. Again, we *have* to be able to go beyond the constant babble of the conscious mind in order to reach unseen worlds and unseen levels.

Unseen Beings, Unseen Worlds

*"What I must do is all that concerns me,
and not what people think."*

— Emerson

Chapter 10

The Wee People

This book wouldn't be complete unless I made some mention of the mysterious Wee People. They are also known as Gentry, Banshees, Gentle Folk, Fairies, Sidhes, Leprechauns, Elves, Gnomes, Corrigans, Tylwyth Teg, Sith, Daoine Maithe, Ankou and others. I am going to lump them all into one category because I think they all originate from basically the same place. I have no idea where that place is (and neither does anyone else), unless it is some mysterious dimension or octave somewhere, populated by phantom-like life forms. In all of my research, I have run across only three or four people who have had reliable, direct encounters with this enigmatic element of the paranormal. In modern times, at least, since 1920 or so, there seems to have been little activity by the Gentry. I don't know why this is but perhaps on their level they were ordered to have less contact with us humans. Contact between them and us has always been pretty much accidental anyway.

In earlier days, mainly in the 1600s through the 1800s human-

Gentry contact was rather common and it seems it was quite well documented. These contacts were not always beneficial for humans. Even though there are credible instances of Gentry saving the lives of humans or aiding humans in times of famine or financial or physical or mental stress, there are many more credible instances of open conflict with the Gentry. These conflicts were often initiated by a human farmer or peasant who had done something to upset a Gentry. There are many tales of mysterious mishaps and deaths of humans as the result of contact with a member of the Gentry. This conflict was often brought about by a human or humans disturbing or destroying a Gentry's "turf." Evidently, even cutting the wrong bushes in a Gentry's turf was reason enough for retaliation by the Banshees. Just about all of them were capable of great good or great evil. All, that is, except for the wispy little, transparent-winged Tinker Bell-like fairies; they seemed to be only curious, kind and benevolent.

There are a number of books that focus on the Gentry phenomenon but perhaps the best of all is the 524-page scholarly work by W.Y. Evans-Wentz, *The Fairy Faith in Celtic Countries*, first published in 1911 as a thesis presented to Oxford University by Evans-Wentz during his doctorate studies at that English institution. The other book, *The Secret Commonwealth of Elves, Fauns and Fairies*, published in 1621 and written by the Rev. Robert Kirk, is still in print and is regarded as one of the best ever on the subject.

The following wee people example is an excerpt from my monthly magazine column in the widely distributed *Sedona Journal of Emergence*. It is from the September 1993 issue.

"There is nothing about the supernatural, high strangeness or paranormal worlds that is boring. It is an endlessly exciting subject.

Doing the kind of research that I do, I constantly run across things that are extraordinarily unusual. Lately, for my new book *Unseen Beings, Unseen Worlds*, I have been doing a bit of research into Fairies, Leprechauns, Elves, Gnomes, Banshees and Sidhes. All those and "ghosts" and UFO/alien activity are directly and indirectly connected. One thing often links to another by extremely curious threads or coincidences, as is the case in all paranormal activity.

The Wee People

A retired lady in Sacramento has graciously sent me several letters describing some of the out-of-the-ordinary experiences she has had in her lifetime. She is obviously a very intelligent woman, judging by the tone of her letters, and she has had a number of odd occurrences happen to and around her. I always wonder why it is that certain people, for no discernible reason, seem to be singled out to experience or be shown *highly* paranormal activity.

One of this woman's first experiences was when she was a little girl. This is a slightly edited excerpt from one of her letters:

"...and when I was around five years old I captured a little man in a backyard tomato patch. The tomato patch belonged to our attic tenant, an old Italian woman. The little man looked very much like the Mickey Rooney of today. He was dressed in handsome, well-made clothes. He had on a white shirt, green vest, green knee-pants, white knee-length socks and shiny black shoes with silver buckles. I grabbed him. He struggled and cussed me out in gibberish. I carted him into the house where my father—shaken to the core—ordered me to let him go. The little man scampered out the door and was barely able to climb the few steps leading back down into the yard."

If you were a little man, maybe a foot and a half tall, door steps would seem like a series of three-foot cliffs.

The following account is of an episode with the Wee People that occurred nearly a hundred years ago. Notice the similarity to the Sacramento woman's encounter. This is excerpted from *The Fairy Faith in Celtic Countries* by W. Y. Evans Wentz:

"There is some of this feeling too in that strange story reported by Lady Archibald Campbell in 1907, when she spoke with an old blind man and his wife living in an Irish glen who claimed to have (caught) a fairy and kept it captive for two weeks — a little red-capped fellow, not two feet high, his hair reddish, his skin very clear but dark in color. The little red cap fitted neatly upon his head. His dress was green, soft to the touch, shorter than a kilt; his boots were as soft as moss over his naked legs. It was a Leprechaun — the fairy that might bring luck to a poor man, for he knows where the crocks of gold are hidden:

'I gripped him close in my arms and took him home. I called to the woman (*his wife*) to look at what I had got. "What doll is it you have there" she cried. "A living one," I said, and put it on the dresser. We feared to lose it; we kept the door locked. It talked and muttered to itself queer words...It might have been near on a fortnight since we had the fairy, when I said to the woman, "Sure, if we show it in the great city we will be made up." (*i.e., become rich*). So we put it in a cage. At night we would leave the cage door open, and we would hear it stirring through the house...we fed it on bread and rice and milk out of a cup at the end of a spoon...

"But finally it got away and they had had bad luck ever since, the old man said sadly: 'For me, though I've lost my sight, the day I took the Leprechaun I thought no harm, only that we would be made up. I am thinking different now by the way things have gone. Sure, we are among them in God's world who are born to be poor."

The Sacramento woman's experience is not unique, by any means. There have been thousands of encounters like this over the years by people all over the world. The Smithsonian Institution has the perfectly preserved body of a sixteen-inch-tall person found when miners blasted through solid rock looking for gold. The little man was discovered sitting on a rock ledge in an ancient cave. An autopsy showed that his anatomy was identical to that of a modern full-grown human. His clothed body may have been entombed in the space for untold millions of years.

In a sadder case of contact with the little people, only a few years ago two farmers in Texas were one day doing some work out in a field. The men had their dogs with them and suddenly the dogs started barking furiously at something they had come across in the woods at the edge of the field. The farmers thought it was probably just the usual raccoon or an opossum but the dogs were unusually excited, so the men stopped their work and went to see just what the commotion was about.

The two men got the shock of their lives when they came up to the hysterically barking dogs. Sitting on a fallen branch between the two dogs was a very small man, about twenty inches tall. The tiny man was sitting there calmly with an expression of complete resignation

The Wee People

on his face. He obviously knew he was trapped and could do nothing. The stunned farmers paused for a few moments, still unable to believe what they were seeing—then the dogs attacked the little man. They tore him to pieces. It was over in seconds.

The farmers watched, still unable to act or to believe what they saw. They turned and went back out into the field and silently resumed work. Several times that day, still not able to believe what they had seen, they went back to look at the tiny human body parts and bloody ground. Finally accepting what had happened, they contacted the local sheriff. The two men took the sheriff to the location of the attack. There were patches of blood and signs of violence but all parts and traces of the little man had mysteriously vanished. That was the beginning and end of that particular human-wee people episode. As I said, there have been many.

Getting back to another of the lady's letters...one night she was working a late shift in a hospital in California:

"I was up late reading, again waiting for the nurses to come in. My door was locked and bolted to be safe, when I caught sight of a bunch of smoke that had gathered over near the door. I wondered how cigarette smoke could bunch up like that when the last cigarette was well out and the smoke gone. So I turned my head for a better look.

"The smoke seemed to be consolidating. Then a beautiful lady emerged. She had a great mop of golden hair that fell to her mid-back. Her skin was pearly white, her eyes of a pale blue or grey. She had an exquisite body, was about 5 feet 7 inches, and she was dressed in a chiffon-like garment of an ancient Grecian style—one bare shoulder, a bodice, then three layers of flouncy pleats or gatherings. She may have been bare of foot. As she gracefully went by, she seemed to put a finger to her lips as if to say, 'Shhh, be quiet.'

"My heart pounded and shock waves went up and down my body. The lady went to the same window (where I had seen the UFO) and faded through it. Next, a big wave of sleep knocked me back into my pillows."

Out of the same window the apparition had gone through the woman had seen, just nights before, a very large UFO that had flown right over Redwood City, California. The UFO had emitted a machine-like vibration as it passed over the hospital, but only a few people reported the sighting because it was in the early hours of the morning. Were the two events connected? I believe they were.

Unseen Beings, Unseen Worlds

*"Death is no more than a separation
of the body from the soul, which is
immortal and imperishable. And at death,
the guardian spirit who is allotted to each
man for life, leads him to his proper
dwelling place according to the life
he has lived on earth."*

— Socrates (469 - 399 B.C.)

Chapter 11

ETs and Others

Primarily my focus is and has been that of a researcher of the extreme paranormal but with a major portion of my time spent on UFOs and alien research. I have written so much about UFOs and aliens before in my other books and various writings I am going to touch on the topic only briefly here. Based on what I have learned pursuing the unusual, I am certain that all paranormal, high strangeness and supernatural worlds, including UFOs and aliens, are somehow connected by an enormously curious thread. This thread runs through and connects anything and everything that is beyond our assumed range of perception. If I am correct about this it is all the more reason why we need to break free of our physical restrictions and join the advanced worlds Out There. All of us. Won't it be interesting when the veils are down and we can interact freely with the higher worlds and see for ourselves what is really truly Out There!

We as Earth humans have so enmeshed ourselves in tribal warfare, materiality and de-evolutionizing, nonprogressive, almost reverse thinking for so long that we have unknowingly and willfully kept ourselves separate from the more finite and infinite worlds that exist all around us. And in a sense we have kept ourselves vulnerable through ignorance. It would be to our infinite advantage to connect with and join, with as little mysticism as possible, those who possess far greater wisdom and knowledge than we do.

Most alien life forms seem to be humanoid or to have at one time been humanoid, but that is probably the only thing that they consistently have in common. By humanoid I mean they have one head, two arms, two hands, two feet and two eyes—the same basic form as we have. There are, I think, in our cosmic vicinity, around two dozen completely different humanoid species of "aliens," and it's possible that there are dozens of related subspecies of that two dozen. There may be more, there may be fewer, but two dozen is a good working estimate. I gather that the most unusual, or bizarre, of these many species are the aliens who must have evolved from reptiles. They are humanoid, like us, but have the skin and cat-like eyes of a reptile. There is also some slim evidence of aliens who evolved from insects, namely the praying mantis. Many, if not all of these higher beings, can materialize at will into and out of our Earthly dimension.

The reptilian aliens, according to eyewitness accounts, seem to be tremendously advanced intellectually but are machine-like cold and calculating and seem to have few emotions. If we do have alien enemies, and I am now 100% positive that we do, I think the lizard-like reptilians are one of them, probably number one. I think there are two other enemy alien types, one being a race of humans who are in appearance indistinguishable from us. One of them could sit next to you on a bus and you wouldn't notice anything unusual. The third type is one, maybe more, of the small-in-stature, large-eyed aliens.

From the previous sentence if I had to pick two examples of the small-in-stature enemy alien types I would say that one alien is from the group that are three to four feet tall and have lightbulb heads and large almond-shaped eyes. The second alien type would be a small dwarflike alien that is two to three feet tall, is very muscular with humanlike proportions and is extremely hostile.

We indeed have alien friends also, and these alien allies more than offset the presence of the "bad guys." Curiously, our best and closest ally seems to be a human alien group who look just like us. Down through history there is clear evidence of these human alien groups. Read Bramley's *"The Gods of Eden"*. Are these humans in reality a single group with a mission of teaching us some kind of lesson? Who knows? Some of these aliens have bases on Earth and some of these bases are in the highest mountains and at the bottom of the deepest seas, underground. Where do all these aliens come from? Where do they live? Where is home to them? An ultimate surprise may be that a number of aliens live in the same space that we do but in a different dimension that has doorways into our own Earth dimension. Some aliens may not necessarily live thousands of lightyears away out in space in a place like Reticulum, Andromeda or the Pleiades. They may be right here among us. And there are, I suspect, life forms Out There which are hundreds of dimensions or universes away that are unlike anything we could dream of. I have had fleeting, shadowy glimpses of them during some of my "travels".

A few years back there was an interesting story making the rounds among UFO research circles about the reptilian humanoids. It seems that in about 1942 a woman in a high political position who was closely associated with the Rothschilds (a dominant banking family in Europe) went one day, unannounced, to see an elder Rothschild about an important business matter. At the mansion, the woman was about to open a door into a room when she noticed that the door was ajar. She heard, coming from the next room, unearthly strange voices in English which at once alarmed her. Very quietly she pushed the door open a tiny bit more and to her absolute shock she found herself gazing at human like beings who looked more like lizards speaking in this strange voice to several members of the Rothschild family. The conversation was about how to better control the world economy—and us. The story could be disinformation or folklore but it fits in too well with other, similar accounts which are widely separated and have the same tone. So it's probably true.

After a lot of reflection on the subject it seems to me that the higher levels of spirituality and UFO aliens (and angels) are integrally linked together. It all, in effect, may very well be essentially one and the same. Can they materialize and manifest in different places and forms? That particular aspect is one that has confounded me over the years of thinking about and researching the paranormal. If alien beings are so advanced that they can traverse time, space and dimensions, they *must* closely interact with the highest levels of Spirit. Do they at times simply assume various physical identities when they want to or need to? It will be interesting when we find out for sure.

In correlation to this, there is no question in my mind that we are constantly being tested, with intentional deception, by some *very advanced* agency. The testing will cease when we stop looking in the wrong directions. (I know what some of you are thinking and that is that there are at least two thousand pages of material from Ashtar, or whomever, that explain these points to a T, with a period at the end. But personally I will not believe *anything* unless I can prove it to myself on my own, in some way, regardless of the purported source.)

Unseen Beings, Unseen Worlds

Prayer of St. Francis of Assisi
Lord, make me an instrument of Your peace;
Where there is hatred, let me sow love;
Where there is injury, pardon;
Where there is doubt, faith;
Where there is despair, hope;
Where there is darkness, light;
Where there is sadness, joy.

Chapter 12

The Free Thinker and the Future

These days, and especially the coming days, I think should be the era of the unrestrained Free Thinker, an era of free thinking that is detached, indifferent, questioning, loving, spiritual and free of old dogma and conditioning. If each individual would, with no fear, prejudice or preconceived notions, inspect all available sensible literature and make independent, uninfluenced deductions about what is Out There, one would certainly find that his or her conclusions are greatly different from the pre-conditioned ideas the majority of humanity holds as truth. The Free Thinker will not tolerate limitations or the stagnant, cult-like thinking of "old" humanity. The Free Thinker re-owns his or her power and all of Spirit, and the unseen realms respect and honor that. They of the higher realms respect and encourage initiative. I know that last statement to be truth because I have seen it work, over and over, time and time again.

I went to my post office box the other day and in my daily stack of mail there was an interesting letter. It was four pages of neatly typed, articulate and intelligent comment by a fellow in Louisiana who had read my second book, *The Alien Tide* but it was the sort of mail I always can gladly do without. The fellow was a devout Christian fundamentalist and the gist of the long essay was that I was misguided, a tool of demons and surely of Satan himself and that I would probably burn in Hell for eternity for my transgressions and sins. Some people just have no sense of humor. It's encouraging, though, because I *must* be doing *something* right, judging by this fellow's letter and one or two others.

There is an awesome something Out There and it is probably, ultimately, totally beyond our understanding, beyond any real attempt that we could make to understand it. I'm probably talking about God. Any one entity or collection of entities who could create what "It" has is, I think, gropingly incomprehensible to us at our stage of evolution. But any way one slices it, in it there is nothing but wonder, excitement and encouragement. Evolution of the species is obviously part of our existence but by the same token, *all* must have been created in the beginning—life itself and flowers and trees and birds and animals and rocks and fire and humankind and water and so on. We and our science don't really understand what any of these things are; so how can we, at this stage, understand fully the entity or force that created them in the beginning? Any entity who has created such beauty *must* be all-powerful, loving, positive and knowing. I'm sure this entity, or entities, does not want to be worshiped but instead joined with and cooperated with and given the respect due it—with all of our human fantasies left on the doorstep. It can be done and will be done, collectively.

I hope that what I have written in this book underscores a genuine need to approach a better, both-feet-on-the-ground understanding of the unseen worlds and the diverse beings who inhabit those worlds. Our future survival may very well depend on it.

In closing this book I must add a word of caution. Anyone who is prone to paranoia or has strong beliefs about dark forces and such, should probably not try the spirit contact or remote viewing exercises I have included. Our worst enemy is fear itself. Perhaps for the time being, this book can be regarded simply as entertainment.

The Free Thinker and the Future

Humanity does indeed have a glowing, golden future. And as the old saying goes, it's better to be on the train than under it.

See you on the train!

Unseen Beings, Unseen Worlds

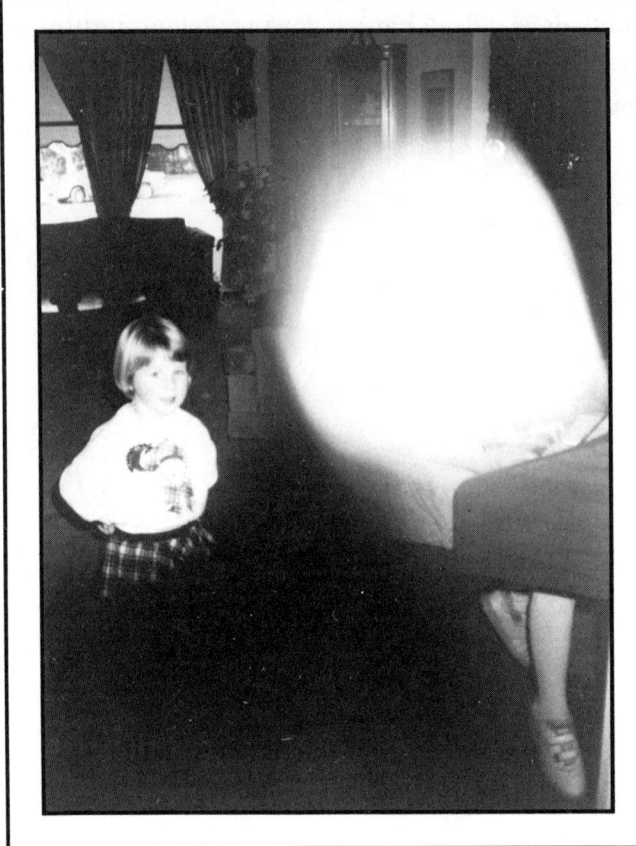

Photo courtesy of Paula Voegler

This photo is unusual by itself but added to that is the fact that the young woman (at right, seated at the piano) has extraordinary psychic abilities. The photo was taken in 1992 when she was twenty years old. By choice she has always been a strict vegetarian. Her mother reports that when her daughter is ill she gets a bowl of water and places a lighted candle beside it and stares at it for as long as an hour — and gets well. No one taught her to do this; she has done this ritual automatically and intuitively all her life. As a child she would often go outside and look wistfully toward the stars and occasionally would say something like, "We are going to the stars together someday — to dance and sing." This sort of longing and stargazing activity has been reported around the world by those who have remarkable children. Starseeds, perhaps?

Photographs

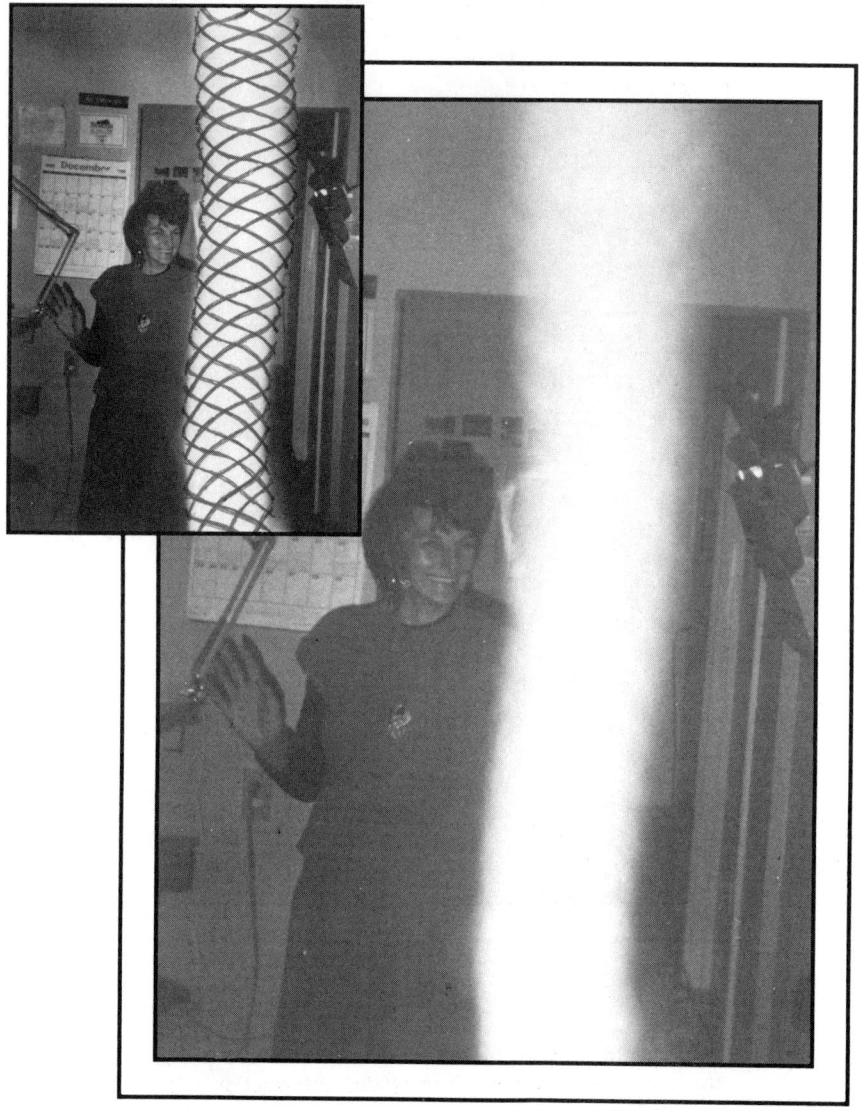

Photo courtesy of Martha Bada

This photo of Sharon Davis, a psychic residing in Sedona, Arizona, was taken about 1990 by Martha Bada, also a Sedona psychic. It's interesting to note that highly paranormal activity depicted in unusual photographs often involve those who have heightened psychic abilities. The inset (top left) shows the spiral pattern (traced in ink) which is visible in the unretouched photo at right.

Unseen Beings, Unseen Worlds

Photo courtesy of Martha Bada

Another photo taken by Martha Bada is of Dove Danu, also a Sedona psychic. (See related information with Sharon Davis photo.)

I believe these spiral-type images are spirits, who are living entities moving at fantastic speeds. A shutter speed of about 1/1600 of a second is required to "catch" one of these spirits — or perhaps more accurately, to photograph their energy trail in a more stationary form. At a very high shutter speed, the spirals usually resemble a thick, white, tightly woven nylon rope.

Photographs

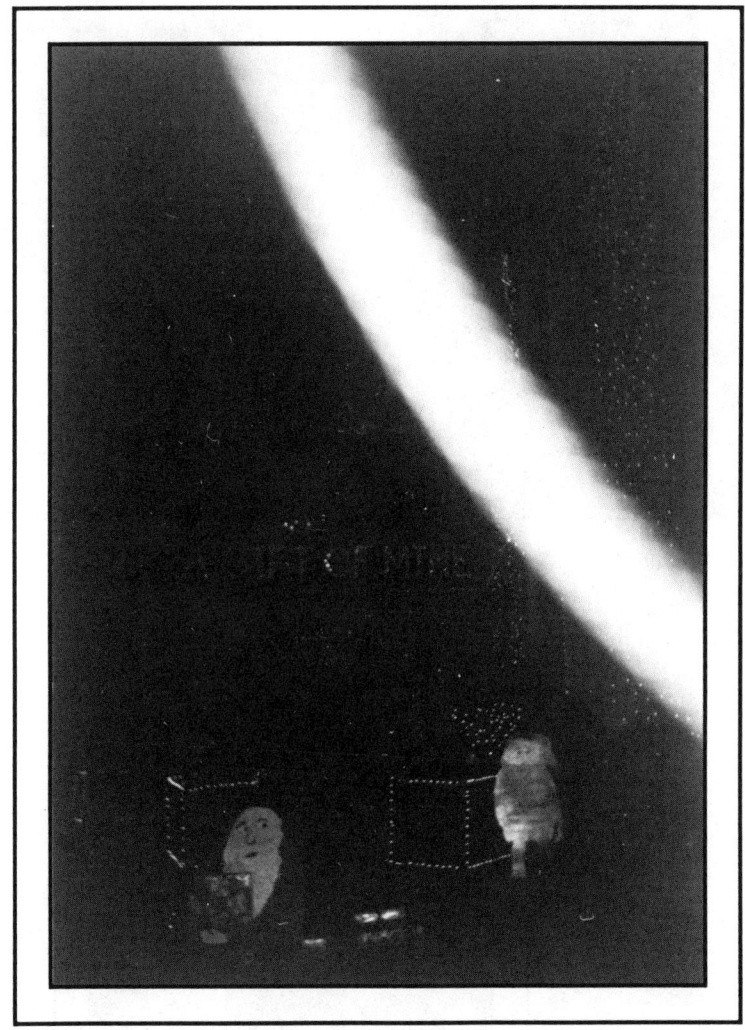

Anonymous

Nighttime Christmas exhibit in Sedona, Arizona, Christmas Eve, 1993

Unseen Beings, Unseen Worlds

Photo courtesy of Christine Wong

(Above) Photo by Christine Wong, a psychic reader in Kaneohe, Hawaii.

Photo courtesy of Roger Bollinger

Photographs

Anonymous

These photos were taken in Tucson, Arizona. The subjects in the photos are masked by their request.

Unseen Beings, Unseen Worlds

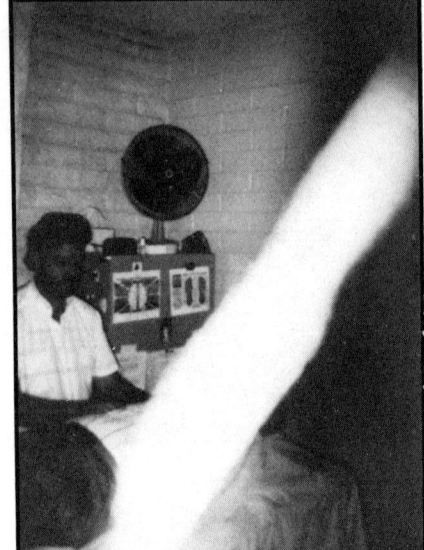

Photos of Roger Bollinger, a hands-on healer, who reports that he has a spirit helper assisting him with his healing practice in Phoenix, Arizona. He often feels the spirit near him when he is healing.

Photos courtesy of Roger Bollinger

Photographs

Photo courtesy of Tom Dongo

This photo was taken by the author over Long Canyon in Sedona, Arizona in 1989 from a helicopter during a time of almost continuous UFO activity in the general area of Long Canyon. Several photos were taken in and around the Sedona area canyons from the helicopter, but it was only in this area that anything unusual showed up on film. These five objects (circled with a paint pen) were not visually seen by the human eye at the time. They are flying in an irregular pattern which eliminates most if not all easy explainable abnormalities in the film, developing, camera or lighting conditions.

Unseen Beings, Unseen Worlds

Photo courtesy of Darelle McCall

I am shown many unusual photographs; the majority of them are usually the result of a flaw in the camera, film or light conditions, etc. When I first saw this photo I rather quickly dismissed it as a fluke or a defect with the film even though Darelle McCall, the woman who took the photo has had a lifetime of extraordinary and very credible alien and UFO encounters. But several weeks later I ran into Darelle and she said she saw something else in the photo — only seen clearly with a magnifying glass (enhanced here so that the "cable" would show up better). Underneath the shiplike object is a clearly definable "cable" that comes out of the bottom of the ship, goes in between two high power lines, and *wraps around* a high power line near a tower crossover bar. The photo was shot in 1993 at Hoover Dam on the Colorado River on the Arizona/Nevada border. The object was not visible to the eye at the time the photo was taken. Camera film often records objects that the human eye will not.

Photographs

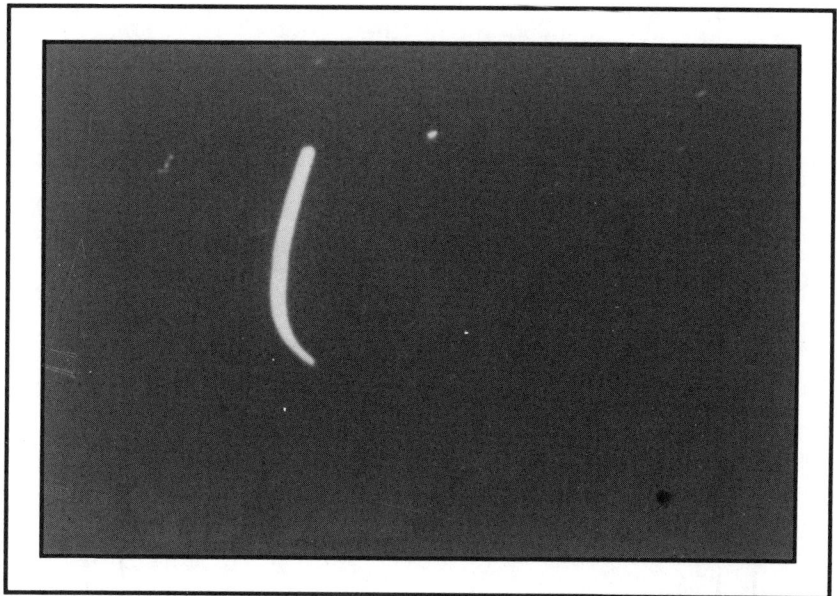

Photos courtesy of Gunter Kaack

These are time-lapse telephoto photographs of moving objects in the night sky over northern Germany.

Unseen Beings, Unseen Worlds

Photo copyright 1993 by Gayle S. Godfrey

This is one of the most extraordinary photographs I have ever seen, and I have seen many. The photo has been thoroughly checked by a photo lab; defects in the film, camera, or developing have been ruled out. The object was photographed near Nogales, Arizona in 1992. It is my opinion that it may be an extremely rare photo of one of the "living" UFOs, an amoeba-like creature that travels through and across dimensions and time.

Photographs

These three photos are of a craft that was reportedly shot down in 1983 over the Caucasus Mountains in Russia by a Soviet-guided missile. Sheepherders who saw the craft come down said that three humanoid beings exited from the craft through the seven foot high hatch or door, seen partially open in the close-up photo. No one seems to know the fate of the humanoids. Six days after the craft landed, the Soviet army removed the strange vehicle.

Notice the man in the top photo is standing on a girder, which was pushed under the craft in order to lift up the craft and transport it. The presence of a man indicates that the photo was not taken on the moon or some other planet. It's also quite obvious that a ship of this design could not fly in our atmosphere by normal means of propulsion which largely eliminates Earth/human origin.

Photos on this page anonymous

Unseen Beings, Unseen Worlds

Photo courtesy of Tom Dongo

This photo was shot by the author in 1991 at Bell Rock in Sedona, Arizona. Bell Rock is world-renowned for its strange psychic and paramormal/supernatural occurrences. Many photos taken around Bell Rock have had unusual objects that mysteriously appear on developed film. Such objects are usually not visible to the human eye when the photo is taken. In this instance the jet contrail (upper left) crosses below the delta-shaped object in the left corner.

Photo courtesy of Wendy O'Brien

The woman who took this photo in 1989 in Cornville, Arizona reported poltergeist-type activity shortly after moving into their newly purchased home, such as strange noises and funiture moving in the night. During a visit I had told Wendy that a resident ghost had been included in the purchase of her house. I felt the ghost was of Spanish origin and harmless. Two days later this object appeared on a photo taken of the back yard.

Photographs

Anonymous

This picture was taken near the Airport vortex on Airport Mesa in Sedona, Arizona about 1985. I've shown this photo to photographic experts and there is no easy explanation that it might be some sort of flaw in the camera, film or developing. What makes the photo even more dramatic is the fact that a number of extremely unusual photos similar to this have been taken on or near the same spot on Airport Mesa. The photos are not all alike but all have light effects such as this photo has. The light effects are not always the same shape or color.

Unseen Beings, Unseen Worlds

Photo courtesy of Lyssa Royal

This remarkable photo was shot in 1992 by a Japanese tourist in Long Canyon in Sedona, Arizona. Long Canyon is known for spectacular UFO and paranormal activity. Much of what I wrote about in my book, *The Alien Tide*, occurred within the general area of where this photo was taken.

Photo courtesy of Lou Hearon

The photo above was taken in Sedona Arizona in the early morning hours about 1989 by a woman who had an irresistible urge to get out of bed, go outside and snap a photo on a pitch dark night with no moon present. When the photo was developed, this object of approximately two hundred yards across appeared on the print. Notice the light diffusion; there is not a central source of light. And whatever it is, it radiated enough energy to provide a lens flare at the bottom right of the photo.

Photo courtesy of Cee Cee Clark

This photo came in my mail just days before this book went to press. It had to be part of this book. Both photos on this page were taken near the Chapel of the Holy Cross in Sedona, Arizona. The object in the photo is metallic and cone shaped on top with a slightly rounded base. It is approximately six feet in diameter and seems to be about one hundred yards from the camera. It is either firing a beam at the ground or leaving an ionization trail (like a jet contrail). There is also a distinct shadow to the right of the beam. It had rained heavily that day. Much more examination will be done on this amazing photo.

Unseen Beings, Unseen Worlds

Photo courtesy of Uilani Singleton

This is a flash photo shot with a Polaroid camera in Sedona's Boynton Canyon in 1991. In the background is an Indian medicine wheel temporarily constructed by devotees of Indian lore. Boynton Canyon is renowned for Indian (past life?) related psychic phenomenon or "flashbacks" by a wide range of visitors. In this photo something in front of the camera reflected back to the film and it strongly suggests either something alien or perhaps an Indian woman with a baby strapped on her back in a carrier.

Photographs

Photo courtesy of Aileen Garoutte

This object appeared on the photo of a sunset taken in Seattle, Washington in 1990 by Aileen Garoutte. Aileen is the director of the UFO Contact Center International that is based in Federal Way, Washington. The author (Tom Dongo) is an associate director in the UFOCCI.

ORDERING BOOKS BY TOM DONGO
Autographed copies

____ **Unseen Beings, Unseen Worlds**   9.95 $ _____

Mysteries of Sedona Series:

____ **Book I — The Mysteries of Sedona**   6.95 $ _____

____ **Book II — The Alien Tide**   7.95 $ _____

____ **Book III — The Quest**   8.95 $ _____

Please include first-class postage & handling as follows: $2.00 for the first book, $1.00 each thereafter. $ _____

TOTAL ENCLOSED $ _____

These rates apply to the U.S.A. only. For orders outside the U.S. please write for rates.

Name _____

Address _____

City _____ State _____ Zip _____

Send your check or money order to:

Mysteries of Sedona
P.O. Box 2571
Sedona, AZ 86339